HERE'S WHAT REVIEW
DAWN HALL'S TWO PREVIOUS COOKBOOKS . . .

"Great for the working family and those on the go."

~ Lori L. Scovel
Manchester Press

"I love Dawn Hall, no doubt about it. Her book reads like a novel, and her life should be a Movie of the Week."

~ Eric Bergeson
The Athens Observer, Athens, GA

"Her dishes were an absolute hit. We are fans of Hall's cookbook and believe it just may be one of the best low-fat cookbooks around."

~ Theresa Campbell
The Herald Bulletin, Anderson, IN

"Dawn Hall could be a poster child for *Good Housekeeping* or *Better Homes and Gardens*."

~ Karen Zielinski
Healthy Living News, Sylvaina, OH

"Dawn's cookbook has stacked up honors."

~ Scott Harrup & Joel Kilpatrick
News Digest

"Delightful cookbook."

~ Diane Eggleston
Elkart Truth, Elkart, IN

"This cookbook author not only has a winning cookbook, but the story behind her foray into the publishing world is an inspiring one."

~ Susan Lockhart
Local Flavor-Northern
Wyoming Daily News

"Dawn's personal book is the perfect solution for on-the-go, health-conscious families."

~ Jane Hall
Vicennes-Sun-Commercial

"The Halls are an ordinary family trying to overcome extraordinary odds. It is a very touching and inspirational story."

~ Betty E. Stumbo
Tribune-Courier, Ontario, OH

"Big oaks grow from little acorns; Dawn Hall, author of the successful self-published 'Down Home Cooking Without the Down Home Fat' has simplified classic heartland recipes for the working person in the soon-to-be released 'Busy People's Low-Fat Cookbook'."

~ JoAnn Livingston
Ennis Daily News, Ennis, TX

2ND SERVING

OF BUSY PEOPLE'S

LOW-FAT Recipes

FOR THE NEW MILLENNIUM

BY AWARD
WINNING AUTHOR

DAWN
HALL

10% of the author's profits from this book will go to Toledo's Solid Rock Outreach Program, focusing on the needs of inner-city children. On behalf of the children, the author thanks you for your support.

ISBN#0-9649950-4-2
Library of Congress Catalog Card Number 99-093352

Copyright © 2000
by Dawn Hall
5425 South Fulton-Lucas Road
Swanton, Ohio 43558

Published by
Cozy Homestead Publishing, Inc.
5425 S. Fulton -Lucas Road
Swanton, Ohio 43558

Printed in the USA by
WIMMER
The Wimmer Companies
Memphis
1-800-548-2537

TABLE OF CONTENTS

(What's Cookin' In This Book)

DEDICATION

Although I believe all of my books are a gift from God, for which I am forever grateful; it is to my sweet, kind and wonderful daughters, Whitney and Ashley, to whom I dedicate this book.

I love to create with food. For me not to be creative with food would be like asking an artist not to paint, a journalist not to write or a singer not to sing. I am very passionate about food, and I've never made the same thing twice except for chicken noodle soup (when someone in the family is sick) and maybe pot roast and hamburgers or hotdogs a few times, because they are my husband's favorites.

Often when others hear this fact for the first time, they think to themselves, "Boy, wouldn't I love to have her cooking for me!" In all honesty though, how would you like to be a guinea pig 365 days a year? It's not what it's cracked up to be.

My daughters have been faithful critics since they could talk. Their brutal honesty has perfected many of my recipes. At times I wish they weren't so good at critiquing my recipes. Yet, I know when I get two thumbs up from them, that even Siskel and Ebert would agree.

Thank you Whitney and Ashley for your loving support. May I always be able to please your tantalizing taste buds!

 4

Miscellaneous Notes to the Cook

When you see this logo, it means the recipe is child appropriate. Most children will be able to make it with a minimum of adult supervision.

When you see this logo it means the recipe is inexpensive to make.

Calphalon Cookware

Although I am not paid to endorse Calphalon Cookware, I absolutely love cooking with it! I truly believe Calphalon nonstick cookware is definitely the best of the best. I am totally impressed.

If you can afford to treat yourself to something special, I'd encourage you to get the commercial non-stick 10 piece set. This is what I use. Whenever I mention a size of cookware for the stove top or oven, I use Calphalon. To order by phone call their toll free number (800) 809-7276. Email address is www.calphalon.com.

Sugar Substitutes

I do not encourage the use of Equal and NutraSweet, which are registered trademarks of the NutraSweet Company. None of these products have sponsored or are otherwise connected with this publication. However, I feel it is important to provide an alternative for those who are diabetic. For more information, you might call: NutraSweet Hotline 1-800-321-7254.

Brand Names

Most brand names used in this book are registered trademarks and are thus protected by law.

Butter Buds/Butter Buds Sprinkles

This is a boxed butter flavored substitute found in the spice section of most grocery stores. To make liquid Butter Buds, simply follow the directions on the box and add water to one envelope of Butter Buds. One Tablespoon of dry Butter Buds Sprinkles is the same as one packet of dry Butter Buds. Butter Buds 1-800-231-1123

WITH SINCERE APPRECIATION
(Acknowledgment)

There's no way I could publish a book of this caliber without the caring and professional help of many. I'd like to publicly thank each. I will be forever thankful to my faithful friends and family. They never complain about trying another new "creation". They are loyal critics through and through. It's their helpful ideas that perfect recipes. A special thank you to my supportive husband and children.

To my students in my aerobic classes and W.O.W. classes (Watching Our Weight), I thank you for encouraging me, even insisting that I write low-fat cookbooks. If it weren't for your persistence and God's leading I may have never put pen to paper. I may have just kept creating new recipes on a daily basis out of sheer passion for no other reason than our own family's nourishment and enjoyment.

To strangers whom I cherish, who write, call and fax me on a regular basis . . . I thank you. This publishing world is tough! (That's the understatement of the year!) It's been your non-stop flow of letters of appreciation that keep me doing what I do. If I were writing books simply to write books, I would've stopped a long time ago. Knowing my gifts and talents are making a positive difference in the lives of others is what keeps me going.

Saying thank you just doesn't seem like enough to my loyal assistants. Diane Bowman-Yantiss has twinkle fingers and is as speedy as they come. She's our whiz on the computer. Karen Schwanbeck and Liz Torda lovingly watch over me like a mother hen. They keep me organized and are always telling me where to go (in a good way.) Last but surely not least, I want to thank the cutest of our publishing group, Mabelina Jackson. When it comes to testing my ideas in the kitchen she's my right hand man. I love and appreciate each of my assistants very much. I thank God for them daily. I don't know what I'd do without them. They have been nothing but a total blessing.

6

Thank you to my editor Janie McGinnis. Not only is she a good editor, she's a dear and precious friend that I cherish.

To Bert & Associates ... most people say they don't like the way they look in pictures. I on the other hand have to admit, I think Bert is able to make me look better in photographs than I do in real life. He doesn't do trick photography or air brushing to touch up pictures, but somehow his photos compliment me. I appreciate that, especially since my books are sold nationally. Thanks, Bert!

To know and work with the staff of Wimmer is to love them, and I sure do. They are such kind and helpful people to work with. A special thanks to Connie Morgan, Jim Hall, Freddie Strange (who is anything but strange), Tammi Hancock, Dawn Rames, Maureen Fortune, Patti Croft and Nancy Duvall.

To my distributors who believe in the quality of my books, and the integrity of my character; I offer my most heartfelt and deepest appreciation. Thank you for believing in me and my books. There were times when I didn't know if I had what it took for my books to compete with the "BIG BOYS" (Big Publishers), but all of you have believed in me. Words will never sufficiently express how deeply I appreciate all of you. Thank you with all of my heart.

I saved the best for last ... to my loving Lord and Savior I give all the praise and glory for the success of my books. It is not logical that I, (a homemaker with only a high school education, not knowing a thing about publishing, or how to type, or how to use a computer) can self-publish and end up selling hundreds of thousands of books. You know what? God isn't logical.

He has done far greater things through me than I had ever dreamed of, thought of or imagined. The passion I have for creating low-fat foods is a gift from God. What I am doing with my passion to bless others is a gift I give to God. He has totally blessed me with an incredible support system of loving and supportive friends, family and business associates. I am truly blessed and forever grateful.

UPDATE OF
DAWN'S PERSONAL STORY

For those of you who have never heard of Dawn Hall, let me take a brief moment to introduce myself. (For those of you who know our story, you can either bear with me or jump forward to One on One with Dawn.)

The media world and conference leaders find it impressive to introduce me as "Dawn Hall, the awarding winning author of "Down Home Cookin' Without the Down Home Fat" and "Busy People's Low-Fat Cookbook". Both are winners of the Best Book of the Year in the Category of Cooking awarded by The North American Bookdealers Exchange in 1996 and 1998. They proceed to talk about big name shows I've been on and flashy awards I've won and on and on and on.

Yes, I'm thankful for the success, but that does not make me who I am. I think of myself as a homemaker who is doing the best I can to keep my loving husband from needlessly dying of brain cancer.

I probably would have never published my books if it weren't for the fact that my husband was diagnosed with an aggressive brain cancer, the size of a baseball, the day after his 32nd birthday in November of 1994. Even radiation did not make his aggressive cancer any smaller.

For 10 years, before I ever thought of writing books, I was dreaming of recipes in my sleep. I thought surely something was wrong with me. Obviously my food addiction had been incorporated into my dreams. I thought I was doomed. Not only were my waking thoughts consumed with creative ideas of what to do with foods, but my dreams were also. What was wrong with me?

Never in a million years did I ever think my dreams of food would end up being a blessing. However, that's exactly what God has done. He has turned my weakness for food into my strength as an author of low-fat books. It's amazing.

Food was not my only weakness. I often like to talk too much. As a little girl, I distinctly remember my mom and my teacher

scolding me for talking. As an adult, I spend a lot of energy trying to be a better listener and not talking so much. The funny thing is, God once again has used my weakness for His praise and glory. I absolutely love being a guest inspirational or motivational speaker for conventions and large groups . . . especially for women. What I once got in trouble for as a child, I am now asked to do! To top it off, it's also how I help financially support our family.

Isn't God incredible? I often tell people, "If I weren't living this miracle, I'd find it hard to believe." Not only is my husband a living miracle, but my story is miraculous also.

In 1995, I went from being a home schooling homemaker, with a high school diploma, who thought for sure her passion for food was a problem, to an author of low-fat cookbooks, who has won numerous awards. All because my loving husband was told in the spring of 1995 by his oncologist to, "Go home and enjoy spring. There's nothing else we can do (to save your life from the aggressive brain cancer.)"

In the summer of 1995, I wanted my husband to try an experimental treatment out of Houston, Texas with Dr. Stanislaw Burzynski. Our insurance would not pay for the treatment that

cost thousands of dollars monthly, because it was experimental. To pay for his experimental brain cancer treatments I self-published my first cookbook, "Down Home Cookin' Without the Down Home Fat". I published it without knowing how to type, use a computer or knowing anything about publishing. We have never looked back.

My husband, Tracy is doing well. Once paralyzed on his entire left side from a surgery that removed one pound of cancer, he is now strong enough to cycle as many as 30 miles in a day. He is also working full-time. Our story is proof that God is still doing miracles as He was thousands of years ago.

I strongly believe my cookbooks are a gift from God that have helped us raise over $100,000.00 needed for my husband's cancer treatment. Now it's time for my books to help others. You can use any of my award winning cookbooks for your fund-raising, including "Busy People's Low-Fat Cookbook", "Down Home Cooking' Without the Down Home Fat", and this book. For more information, please call us at (419) 826-2665. We'd be glad to help.

If you need encouragement, I want to encourage you. No problem is too big for God. Our lives were literally turned inside-out and upside-down. I couldn't figure it out, but God did. To this day I am in awe that my husband is alive and we haven't lost our home. I would never, ever, ever want to go through all we've been through again. At the same time I am totally thankful for all of the good that has been derived from our challenges. We are living examples of triumphing over tragedy with God's help. You can, too.

If you would like to know more about having a personal relationship with God, we will be happy to send you the book "The Message of Hope". Simply send $1.00 along with a self-addressed stamped envelope to:

Cozy Homestead Publishing
c/o Message of Hope
5425 S. Fulton-Lucas Road
Swanton, Ohio 43558

ONE ON ONE WITH DAWN

I wish I could tell you I am no longer a food addict, but I definitely am. It's something I struggle with on a daily basis. For people who don't understand what a food addiction is . . . a food addict uses food like an alcoholic would use alcohol. Besides for nutritional reasons, they also use it for a lot of wrong reasons. I tell people there's nothing a hot fudgie brownie couldn't make feel better. I'm a recovering food addict. It's really, really hard for me not to over indulge in food when I'm going through stressful times. It's something I've struggled with for years. I distinctly remember being six years old and feeling very fat in my little shorts. It's a problem I can always remember having as long as my memory exists.

I have learned what triggers my overeating. I am able to keep it under control, but there are still times that I definitely struggle.

I do the 12 steps of Overeaters Anonymous. I strongly encourage anyone who fears they may be an over-eater or food addict to join a self-help support group. There are wonderful groups that will help you be accountable such as TOPS (Taking Off Pounds Sensibly), Overeaters Anonymous, Weigh Down Workshop, and First Place. I have found for myself it is important to have accountability.

Weight Watchers is also another wonderful group for account-ability for people who have problems with their eating. However, they do charge a weekly fee.

If you have a problem, the first step toward healing is admitting the problem. Being a recovering food addict is different from being a recovering alcoholic. You can't go cold turkey with food like you can with alcohol. People with the best intentions can still struggle. Wouldn't it be nice if we could just bring about whatever desires we wish and it was that simple?

Here are frequent comments made by people who don't have a clue how challenging it is for a recovering food addict such as myself. Well, if you don't want to overeat then just stop eating when you are full . . . just stop thinking about food . . . how about the old standby, if you don't want to be fat then just don't eat fat. People who say these things will never be able to understand

11

the daily struggles we endure as food addicts.

What's important is not that other people understand, but that we ourselves acknowledge our problem. We admit our problem and ask God for help. We do the best we can moment to moment with the help of God. Let's encourage ourselves to remember God is bigger than any problem we have.

When you back slide with your overeating just acknowledge your mistake, pick yourself back up by your boot straps, dust yourself off, and do the best you can to start over again. Try not to be too hard on yourself. As a recovering food addict, I know that sometimes when I struggle, I just want to cry out to God. It says in the Bible that its during the hard times that we grow. Sometimes I just want to cry out to God, "I've grown enough! It's time for a break!"

Cancer, heart disease and diabetes all thrive on a high-fat diet. Even if you do not need to lose weight I strongly encourage you to eat a low-fat, high-protein, low-sugar, lifestyle. Notice I called it a lifestyle not a diet. The reason I did that, is because people think of a diet as deprivation or starvation. Think of it as a lifestyle. Something you choose to do to be a happier, healthier you. I strongly encourage those of you that are into the high-fat diets such as the Atkins diet, only do it under a doctors supervision. In all honesty do you really think God grew all these wonderful fruits, vegetables, grains, legumes, and beans for us not to eat them? I really don't think so.

Studies have shown that people who exercise first thing in the morning are the ones that stick with it. Again, I would like to strongly encourage you to get in the habit of exercising first thing in the morning. We all have those kinds of days, we are going to exercise and we don't. A perfect example would be a day like this . . . we wake up and are pretty tired and decide to sleep just a half hour longer which would have been our exercise time. Then we realize we have crammed too much into our time to get ready by the time we get the children ready for school and lunches packed, we don't have enough time to exercise. So we tell ourselves we will exercise during our lunch hour. At work we get overloaded and we don't have time to exercise during our lunch hour. We then tell ourselves we will exercise after work. After

work we realize all of the errands we have to do and we decide we will exercise once we get home. Once we get home and we are preparing dinner there are so many things coming at you you simply don't have time to exercise so you'll exercise after dinner. After dinner you help with the dishes and help the children with homework, you say you will exercise right before you go to bed. Before bed you are so tired you say you'll exercise tomorrow. I know, I've been there and the cycle of the whirlwind continues on and on and on.

Studies show that people who are overweight tend to be what are called "people pleasers". We are real good at taking care of everyone else and we take care of ourselves last. God tells us to treat others as we would like to be treated. He does not tell us to treat others better than we treat ourselves.

Let us never forget our bodies are a temple of God. I encourage you to take time to take care of yourself. If we are too busy to take care of ourselves then we are too busy! If we do not make it a priority to take care of ourselves then no one else is going to make it a priority. We need for our children to see us taking care of ourselves. We need to be a living example for them. If they see us not taking care of ourselves, then they will grow up and not take care of themselves. If they see us sitting around eating in front of the TV, they are going to grow up sitting around eating in front of the TV. If they see us not exercising, they are going to grow up to not exercise. The Bible tells us to train your children in the way they should go. I believe it is about more than just spiritual things. I believe it is also true about physical and financial. Let us be a living example to our children. Exercise together. Let us walk together, let us cycle together, let us play games together, like softball and volleyball.

We do not have to spend a lot of money on fancy equipment to be healthy or to exercise. We can simply march in place bringing your knee up to hip height for a good half hour in the morning and at the same time you could journal, watch TV or do your daily devotional. Marching in place is good aerobic exercise. If that is not enough exercise for you, then you can pump your arms at the same time.

Both my first and second books "Down Home Cookin' Without the Down Home Fat" and "Busy People's Low-Fat Cookbook" (which won 1996 and 1998 Best Books of the Year in the Category of Cooking by the North American Bookdealers Exchange) teach a lot about an overall healthier lifestyle. Because I have already shared those things with you in the first two books I'm not going to repeat it in this book. However, if you need help learning how to live a healthier lifestyle and not live on a diet please do not hesitate to call (888) 436-9646. In both of my books (just mentioned) I share everything from how to cut the fat, to how to exercise, to how to save a lot of money on your coupons and your groceries, and how to organize your coupon book. There's a lot of information that will be very helpful to someone who has not already made the switch to wanting a healthier lifestyle. For those who've already made the switch, there's still a lot of helpful information you may not have known of. There are over 240 time-saving, homestyle, low-fat recipes in each book, and there are no duplicates in any of the books.

The key is to be in balance. God has given us each our own style, our own personalities, and our own physique. We look at models, TV magazines and the media stereotypes of what is reality. In all actuality these skinny twig type women are very far from reality. The average woman is approximately 5' 4" and weighs 145 pounds. The average woman is not 6' and 125 pounds, as advertisers would like us to believe. The reasons I share these facts with you, is to help us keep in mind what reality really is. Sometimes some of us get discouraged when we order clothing from magazines and it does not look the way it did on the models.

What is important is that we do the best we can to be the healthiest we can be. A lot of us are built like oak trees and we complain our whole lives because we want to be a pine tree. Think of how ridiculous that is. Can you imagine an oak tree complaining because it wants to be built like a pine tree? For a hypothetical example, the oak would complain to God, "I wish I were a pine tree—then I could be used for a Christmas tree and have beautiful lights put on me." All along the oak tree was not appreciating the special tree God had made it.

While the oak tree was complaining, the pine tree was also complaining to God. The pine tree would cry out to God, "Oh God I wish I could be an oak tree so people could sit underneath me and have picnics and enjoy my shade". Think of how ridiculous that is. Neither tree can really appreciate what they are because they are wishing they could be something else.

Often that is what many of us do. If we have curly hair, we wish we had straight and if we have straight hair, we wish it were more curly. If we are skinny we wish we had an hour glass shaped figure. If we have an hour glass shaped figure we wish we were more slender. And the cycle goes on and on and on. We are robbing ourselves of our own joy by not appreciating who we are or how God had made us.

More important than what the scale says or the size of your clothing, is the size of your heart. On a daily basis we need to ask ourselves "Are we living healthy? Are we eating healthy? Are we exercising daily?"

The number one factor in our build is genetic. Numerous studies have been done on twins who have been separated at birth and reunited in their adult life, at the ages of 30, 40, and 50. Researchers were amazingly astounded at the very strong similarities the twins had in their body build. We can try our very best to be healthy. We definitely should. At the same time let's not fight mother nature and strive to be something we are not.

Let's have our goal to be healthy, happy individuals. Make it a priority to be healthy, not only physically, but spiritually, emotionally and mentally. Overall well being and overall good health is a lot more than just the physical. It includes all aspects of our lives.

What I Like to Stock in My Kitchen

There are literally hundreds (if not thousands) of fat-free and very low-fat products on the market today. The problem (as I'm sure a lot of you know) is that many do NOT taste good! Once I tried a new fat-free potato chip. Yuck! I'm telling you, the bag it was packaged in had to taste better than the product! It was terrible!

Eating low-fat really shouldn't be a tasteless, boring experience. My motto regarding low-fat foods is, "if it doesn't taste good don't eat it." There are too many delicious choices available for any of us to waste calories on food that doesn't taste good.

Have no fear! The following is a list of products I enjoy using. An asterisk (*) in front of the product means the generic brands of these items are less expensive and good. Look for them in your grocery store, and have confidence they will taste better than the packaging!

An easy rule of thumb when reading labels: if it has more than 3 grams of fat per 100 calories, don't buy it, don't use it, and pitch it! The only time I break that rule is for super lean beef such as:

Type of Beef	Serving: Size	Fat Grams	Calories	% Fat Calories
London Broil/ Flank Steak	3 oz.	6	167	32%
Top Loin (Lean Only)	3 oz.	6	162	33%
Eye of Round (As a steak, roast or have butcher grind for super lean hamburger)	3 oz.	5	150	30%

If you enjoy eating red meat and do not want to refrain, then I encourage you to make the switch to ground eye of round. You'll be doing your heart, health, and waistline a lot of good!

The second time I break the rule is when I "choose to wander." An example might be a small piece of chocolate. Remember, this is done very rarely!

(Note: I am not a big fan of fat-free cheeses or margarines, but in my recipes, they taste good.)

Butter & Margarines

Butter Buds
(found in spice or diet section)

Butter-flavored Pan Spray

Non-fat cooking sprays (generic brands are fine)

I Can't Believe It's Not Butter Spray

Ultra Fat-free Promise Margarine

Breads & Grains

Aunt Millie's breads & buns

*Enriched flour

Father Sam's Kangaroo Bread

Flour tortillas fat-free (El Paso and Buena Vista are good)

*Graham crackers

Health Valley fat-free cookies

Health Valley fat-free granola (I use for my homemade granola bars)

*Italian seasoned bread crumbs

Lite breads with 40 calories and no fat per slice (Aunt Millie's, Bunny, and Wonder are good)

Nabisco Reduced Fat Ritz Crackers

*Oyster Crackers

*Pastas (except egg noodles; pastas from whole durum wheat are best)

Pillsbury Buttermilk Biscuits

Pillsbury Pizza Crust

Quaker Rice Cakes (caramel and strawberry flavored)

Rice (whole grain enriched)

Rightshape Biscuits (buttermilk flavor)

Vegetable bread

*Whole grain and white rice

*Whole wheat flour

Beverages

*Bottled water (don't be fooled by flavored waters; a lot of them are loaded with sugar and calories)

*Cider

Country Time Lemonade
(sugar free)

Crystal Light (sugar free)

Dole fruit juices (100%)

*Grapefruit juice (100%)

Kool-Aid (sugar free)

*Orange juice (100%)

*Prune juice (100%)

Tea (instant or tea bag)

*Tomato juice

Virgin Mary juice

Cheese
**(To be honest with you, I do
not like fat-free cheese, but
used properly in recipes they
can taste delicious!)**

Borden Fat-Free cheese
slices-Sharp Cheddar flavor

Healthy Choice fat-free
cheese

*Italian topping (grated)

Kraft Fat-Free cheeses -
all flavors

Kraft "Free" Parmesan
cheese

Kroger brands of dairy
products including frozen

*Parmesan (grated)

Sargenta Fat-Free Ricotta

Condiments

A1 Sauce

*Almond extract

Barbecue Sauces
(all - I haven't found one
high in fat)

Braum's fat-free fudge topping

*Cocoa

Coconut extract

*Cornstarch

Equal

Evaporated skim milk (Lite)

Heinz 57 Sauce

Hershey's Lite Syrup

Hidden Valley Fat-Free Ranch
Salad Dressing

Hidden Valley Reduced Calorie
Dry Salad Dressing Mix

*Honey

*Karo Syrup

*Ketchup

Kraft Free Mayonnaise and
Miracle Whip

Kraft Fat-Free Tartar Sauce

Kroger Fat-Free ice cream
toppings

Liquid smoke

*Lite soy sauce

Lite teriyaki marinade

*Lite syrups
(I like Mrs. Butterworth's)

*Mint extract

Mrs. Richardson's fat-free
   ice cream toppings

*Mustard

Not So Sloppy Joe Mix

Nutra Sweet

*Pam non-fat cooking spray

Preserves and jellies
   (low sugar)

Seven Seas "Free" Ranch
   Salad Dressing

Seven Seas "Free" Red Wine
   Vinegar Salad Dressing

Seven Seas "Free" Viva Italian
   Salad Dressing

Smucker's fat-free toppings

T. Marzetti's Fat-Free
   Raspberry Salad Dressing

*Taco seasoning mix

*Tomato sauce

*Vanilla

Western Fat-Free Salad
   Dressing

Flavorite Fat-Free yogurts
   and non-fat cottage cheese

Fleishmann's Fat-Free
   Buttery Spread
   (comes in a bottle)

Fleishmann's Fat-Free Cheese
   Spread (comes in a bottle)

Healthy Indulgence
   (Kroger Not So Sloppy Joe
   Mix grocery stores' name
   brand fat-free cheeses,
   yogurts, etc.)

Pet Fat-Free evaporated
   canned skimmed milk

Reddi Whip Fat-Free Whipped
   Topping

Skim milk

Sour cream-Fat-Free
   (I like Light & Lively or
   Land O Lakes)

Yogurts - Fat-Free
   (watch labels)

Dairy

Buttermilk (non-fat)

*Cottage cheese (non-fat)
   (I like all of them)

*Dry powdered milk
   (non-fat) (best used in
   recipes - I don't care to
   drink it)

Eagle brand Fat-Free
   condensed sweetened milk

Junk Food

Baked Tostitos, Salsa &
   Cream Cheese, Cool Ranch,
   and regular flavors

*Caramel corn
   (krack-o-pop most brands
   are only 1 fat gram but high
   in sugar content which is
   still too much sugar or salt
   to eat a lot of)

Dole fruit & juice bars

Entenmann's fat-free baked goods (Beware! These babies are loaded with sugar!)

Fat-free ice cream

Frito Lay Potato Crisps (new potato chip substitute) (They're delicious - if you like Pringles you'll like these! Only 1.5 grams per 100 calories - about 12 chips)

Frozen fat-free yogurts (T.C.B.Y., Healthy Choice & Kemps)

*Fudge Bars (most are low-fat or fat-free)

Health Valley fat-free tarts

Hostess "Lite" twinkies, cupcakes, brownies, and muffins (all flavors) (It's hard to believe they're really low fat.)

Jello fat-free pudding and pudding cups

Keebler Elfin Delights

Little Debbie's Lite Oatmeal Pies and Brownies

*Marshmallows

*Marshmallow Creme

Pepperidge Farm Fat-Free Brownies and Blondies (too good!)

Pop Secret Popcorn Bars

*Popsicles - all

*Pretzels

Quaker low-fat granola bars

Rice cakes (Quaker strawberry, rice, corn & caramel flavored)

Richard Simmons cookies

Smart Pop microwave popcorn (Orville Redenbacker)

Snack Well's cookies, tarts and breakfast bars

Super Pretzels - soft pretzels

Sweet Escapes Candies (by Hershey's)

*Welch's frozen juice bars

Meats, Fish, Poultry

Beef (eye of round, London broil, flank steak, top loin)

Butter Ball Fat-Free sausage, turkey breast and lunchmeats

Canadian bacon (usually very low in fat)

Chicken breast (no skin; dark meat has twice as much fat!)

Crabmeat flake or stick (imitation)

Eckrich fat-free meats (hot dogs, lunch meats, smoked sausage, kielbasa)

Fish (the white ones are lower in fats; i.e., flounder, grouper, pike, sole, cod, orange roughy, monk fish, perch, scallops)

Healthy Choice lunch meat, hot dogs and smoked sausage

Hillshire Farms Fat-Free smoked sausage & kielbasa

Hotdogs - Healthy Choice - 1 fat gram; Hormel Light & Lean - 1 fat gram; Oscar Mayer Fat-Free

Morning Star Ground Meatless (for chilis, pasta sauces, etc., but not alone as a burger)

Shellfish (Lobster, Crab, Shrimp)

*Tuna (packed in water)

Turkey breast (no skin; dark meat has twice as much fat!)

Pre-Packaged Items

*Applesauce (sugar-free is lower in calories)

Betty Crocker "Lite" Cake, Brownie, Bread & Muffin mixes

*Bouillon cubes (chicken, beef, and vegetable flavors)

Healthy Choice low-fat frozen meals

Hot chili beans (I like Brook's)

Nestle's Fat-Free, sugar free hot chocolate

Simply potatoes shredded hashbrowns (found in refrigerator section)

Swiss Miss Fat-Free, sugar free hot chocolate

Fruits and Veggies

*Canned vegetables - no salt added

*Canned fruits in fruit juice only

*Cranberry sauce

Fresh vegetables - all (except for avocado - major fat!!)

*Frozen vegetables and fruits - all - with no sugar added

*Lite fruit cocktail

*Lite pie fillings - cherry, apple, and blueberry

Other Items

*Bac-O's (imitation bacon bits)

Betty Crocker Reduced Fat Sweet Rewards Cake Mix

Campbell's Healthy Request low-fat & fat-free sauces

Chef Boy-R-Dee Spaghetti O's

Cool Whip Free

Dream Whip

Eggs (use only the whites)

*Egg Beaters

Gold Medal Fudge Brownie Mix

Healthy Indulgence (Kroger's name brand) fat-free cheeses, yogurts, etc,)

Health Valley Chili and Soups

Healthy Choice soups and sauces (low- and no-fat)

*Instant mashed potatoes

Jiffy cake mixes

*Legumes (Beans - canned or dry variety and lentils)

Martha Whites's Lite mixes (muffins, etc.)

Nabisco's "Royal" Lite Cheesecake mixes

Old El Paso fat-free refried beans

*Pancake and buttermilk pancake mix

*Pasta

Pillsbury Lovin' Lites frostings

Progresso "Healthy Classics" soups

Special K Fat-free Waffles

*Stuffing mixes (look for brands that have only 2 fat grams per serving as packaged)

Sauces

Campbell's Healthy Request low-fat & fat-free soups

Healthy Choice Spaghetti Sauce

Heinz Homestyle Lite gravies (in a jar)

Hunts "Light" fat-free pasta sauce

Pepperidge Farm Stroganoff Gravy

Prego spaghetti and pizza sauce (Lite ones)

Ragu Lite "Garden Harvest" & "Tomato & Herb"

Ragu Pizza Quick Sauce

Ragu Today's Recipe spaghetti sauces (low fat)

Great Beginnings
Beverages, Appetizers & Breads

HONEY BUTTER

Delightfully tasty! A great spread for toasted bagels or toasted raisin bread.

1 (8-ounce) container fat-free Ultra Promise margarine

¼ cup honey
¼ cup powdered sugar

♥ Beat all ingredients together until fluffy and well blended.

Yield: 21 (1-tablespoon) servings

Calories: 22
Percent Fat Calories: 0%
Carbohydrate: 5 grams
Protein: 0 grams

Total Fat: 0 grams
Cholesterol: 0 mg
Dietary Fiber: 0 grams
Sodium: 70 mg

Menu Ideas: Great on toast or used as a glaze over cooked carrots or peas.

Great Beginnings
Beverages, Appetizers & Breads

Budget Friendly Recipe

Poor Boy's Cappuccino

Kids Cookin'

Craving a cappuccino, but not owning an expensive cappuccino machine and not wanting to pay the high price of the cappuccino mixes, I created this. It's pretty good! If you like BP gas station's cappuccino, you'll like this. Not a true cappuccino, but mighty tasty!

1 cup water
½ teaspoon instant coffee
2 tablespoons powdered fat-free hot cocoa mix

1 tablespoon of your favorite flavor nondairy fat-free creamer (Coffee Mate)

♥ Microwave water for 1 minute or until piping hot.
♥ Stir in remaining ingredients until dissolved and well mixed.

Yield: 1 (1-cup) serving

Calories: 126
Percent Fat Calories: 0%
Carbohydrate: 23 grams
Protein: 6 grams

Total Fat: 0 grams
Cholesterol: 0 mg
Dietary Fiber: 2 grams
Sodium: 432 mg

Menu Ideas: Anytime and anywhere.

Total Time: 5 minutes or less.

Kids Cookin'

BEAN DIP

Budget
Friendly
Recipe

My family likes bean dip, but it's so
expensive! (Approximately $2.50 for 9 ounces.) My
family likes this every bit as much, and it's a fraction of
the cost! The key is to buy the least expensive ingredients
as possible to make this recipe. You can't taste the
difference and you'll save 'mucho moola'! (A lot of money!)

1 (16-ounce) can fat-free
   refried beans

2 teaspoons dry taco
   seasoning mix (same as
   what you'd use to make
   tacos)

♥ Mix ingredients together with a spatula until well blended.
Serve at room temperature. Refrigerate unused portion.

Yield: 20 (2-tablespoon) servings

Calories: 21
Percent Fat Calories: 0%
Carbohydrate: 4 grams
Protein: 1 gram

Total Fat: 0 grams
Cholesterol: 0 mg
Dietary Fiber: 1 gram
Sodium: 95 mg

Cheesy Bean Dip: Make bean dip recipe above exactly the
same, but stir in ½ cup of Cheez Whiz Light.

Before stirring in Cheez Whiz Light, microwave for
approximately 30 to 40 seconds to melt cheese. Then,
stir Cheez Whiz Light into the bean mixture. Serve at
room temperature.

Yield: 24 (2-tablespoon) servings

Calories: 31
Percent Fat Calories: 16%
Carbohydrate: 4 grams
Protein: 2 grams

Total Fat: 1 gram
Cholesterol: 3 mg
Dietary Fiber: 1 gram
Sodium: 170 mg

Menu Ideas: Serve with Baked Tostitos or Baked Bugles.

Budget
Friendly

Recipe

SOUTHWESTERN
REFRIED BEAN DIP

Kids
Cookin'

Great Beginnings
Beverages, Appetizers & Breads

*This thick dip is very rich. When eaten
with Baked Tostitos it is a good source of protein.*

1 (1.25-ounce) package
taco seasoning mix - dry
1 (16-ounce) container
fat-free sour cream

1 (16-ounce) can fat-free
refried beans

♥ Mix taco seasoning mix and sour cream until well blended.

♥ Stir in refried beans.

♥ Serve as is or chilled, with Baked Tostitos.

♥ For those liking spicier foods, add a few drops of Tabasco
sauce to taste.

Yield: 14 (¼-cup) servings

Calories: 72
Percent Fat Calories: 0%
Carbohydrate: 13 grams
Protein: 4 grams

Total Fat: 0 grams
Cholesterol: 3 mg
Dietary Fiber: 2 grams
Sodium: 261 mg

Menu Ideas: Serve with Baked Tostitos.

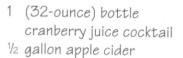

HOLIDAY WARM PUNCH

Delicious to the last drop!

Budget
Friendly

Recipe

1 (32-ounce) bottle
  cranberry juice cocktail
½ gallon apple cider

1 (2-liter) bottle diet
  Mountain Dew (or regular
  Mountain Dew)
1 teaspoon ground
  cinnamon

♥ Bring everything to a boil and boil for 2 minutes.
♥ Serve hot.

Yield: 20 (1-cup) servings

Calories: 76
Percent Fat Calories: 0%
Carbohydrate: 19 grams
Protein: 0 grams

Total Fat: 0 grams
Cholesterol: 0 mg
Dietary Fiber: 0 grams
Sodium: 14 mg

Note: Nutritional information based on diet soda.

**Menu Ideas: Great for warming up after
Christmas caroling or after any cold winter sport.**

Budget
Friendly
Recipe

Honey Mustard
Piggy Dippers

Appetizers can't get much easier than this folks!

½ cup fat-free Marzetti's
honey mustard salad
dressing

1 (14-ounce) package
fat-free smoked sausage
(I use Butterball)

♥ Cut sausage into ½-inch chunks. Mix with salad dressing until well coated.

♥ Cover and cook in carousel microwave for 4 to 5 minutes, or until fully heated.

♥ Serve with toothpicks.

Yield: 7 (2-ounce) appetizer servings

Calories: 87
Percent Fat Calories: 0%
Carbohydrate: 13 grams
Protein: 9 grams

Total Fat: 0 grams
Cholesterol: 24 mg
Dietary Fiber: 0 grams
Sodium: 830 mg

Yield: 4 (3½-ounce) entrée servings

Calories: 153
Percent Fat Calories: 0%
Carbohydrate: 22 grams
Protein: 15 grams

Total Fat: 0 grams
Cholesterol: 43 mg
Dietary Fiber: 0 grams
Sodium: 1453 mg

Menu Ideas: Great for parties.

For parties, make a double batch - keep in crockpot.

HONEY MUSTARD SMOKED SAUSAGE CHEESE SPREAD

Budget Friendly Recipe

*A great snack or appetizer with crackers,
also delicious as a sandwich spread.*

1 (14-ounce) package
fat-free smoked sausage
(I use Butterball)

1 small onion (or ⅓ cup
frozen chopped onion)

2 (8-ounce) packages
fat-free cream cheese -
softened

½ cup fat-free Marzetti's
honey mustard salad
dressing

1 (8-ounce) package fat-
free shredded cheddar
cheese (I use Kraft)

♥ Put everything in a food processor and continue processing
until completely well mixed.

♥ Serve chilled.

Yield: 16 (¼-cup) servings

Calories: 87
Percent Fat Calories: 0%
Carbohydrate: 9 grams
Protein: 13 grams

Total Fat: 0 grams
Cholesterol: 14 mg
Dietary Fiber: 0 grams
Sodium: 608 mg

**Menu Ideas: On crackers as an appetizer,
or on bread for a sandwich.**

*"Marriages don't fail . . .
people do".*

Pastor Doug Clay

Budget
Friendly

Recipe

SMOKED SAUSAGE
CHEESE SPREAD

Really good!

1 (14-ounce) package
   fat-free smoked sausage
   (I use Butterball)
3 (8-ounce) packages
   fat-free cream cheese -
   softened
4 green onions - chopped

½ cup fat-free mayonnaise
   (Do not use Miracle Whip)
½ teaspoon garlic powder
½ teaspoon minced garlic
1 (1-ounce) package Ranch
   dip mix (found in salad
   dressing aisle)

♥ Grind smoked sausage in a food processor until finely
   ground.
♥ Mix all ingredients together with a spatula until well mixed.
♥ Serve with fat-free crackers.

Yield: 28 (2-tablespoons) servings

Calories: 43
Percent Fat Calories: 0%
Carbohydrate: 4 grams
Protein: 6 grams

Total Fat: 0 grams
Cholesterol: 8 mg
Dietary Fiber: 0 grams
Sodium: 432 mg

*Menu Ideas: Good on crackers or
stuffed in celery or cherry tomatoes.*

HAWAIIAN CHICKEN SPREAD

*Budget
Friendly*

Recipe

*Tropical flavors make
this chicken spread unique.*

1 (8-ounce) package
fat-free cream cheese
1 (8-ounce) can crushed
pineapple in its own juice -
drained
1 (5-ounce) can chicken

3 tablespoons fresh
chopped chives
(or 1½ tablespoons dried)
2 tablespoons Kikkoman
Teriyaki Baste and Glaze
(found in barbecue sauce
section)

♥ Mix all ingredients together. Serve chilled.

Yield: 16 (2-tablespoon) servings

Calories: 35
Percent Fat Calories: 19%
Carbohydrate: 3 grams
Protein: 4 grams

Total Fat: 1 gram
Cholesterol: 7 mg
Dietary Fiber: O grams
Sodium: 164 mg

**Menu Ideas: Stuff in celery, spread on crackers
or on toasted bread for a tasty open-faced sandwich.
Stuff in pita bread or spread on a flour tortilla
with leaf lettuce and serve as a wrap.**

Hawaiian Tuna Spread: Make exactly the same, but
substitute one 6-ounce can of tuna for the chicken.

Yield: 16 (2-tablespoon) servings

Calories: 32
Percent Fat Calories: 3%
Carbohydrate: 3 grams
Protein: 5 grams

Total Fat: trace
Cholesterol: 4 mg
Dietary Fiber: O grams
Sodium: 154 mg

Budget
Friendly
Recipe

CRUNCHY VEGETABLE SPREAD

Absolutely delicious and so versatile!

1 (8-ounce) package fat-free cream cheese
1 (8-ounce) container fat-free sour cream
1 (0.59-ounce) package Hidden Valley Ranch dip mix - dry

1 cup chopped celery
1 medium-size red bell pepper - chopped
1 medium-size cucumber - seeded and chopped
¼ cup fresh or frozen chopped onion

♥ With a mixer beat together cream cheese, sour cream and Hidden Valley Ranch dip mix until well blended and creamy.

♥ With a spoon, stir in vegetables until well blended.

Yield: 10 (¼-cup) servings

Calories: 60
Percent Fat Calories: 0%
Carbohydrate: 9 grams
Protein: 5 grams

Total Fat: 0 grams
Cholesterol: 4 mg
Dietary Fiber: 1 gram
Sodium: 334 mg

Menu Ideas: Absolutely delicious on Bagel Chips (page 39), toast, pita sandwiches or as a dip.

If God can get along with only 10% then why can't our government?

I think our government should work with 10% like God does.

Dawn Hall

CHEESE FILLED
SOFT BREAD STICKS

Budget
Friendly

Recipe

*This recipe turns ordinary biscuits
into extraordinary baked goods.*

1 (7.5-ounce) can Pillsbury
  buttermilk biscuits
2 slices sharp cheddar
  Kraft Free singles - each
  slice cut into 5 strips

¼ cup shredded Parmesan
  cheese (I use Kraft) -
  chopped into tiny pieces
Garlic salt - optional

♥ Preheat oven to 425 degrees.

♥ Spray a cookie sheet with non-fat cooking spray.

♥ Make each bread stick **individually** as follows:
   Roll biscuit into a 3½-inch to 4-inch length
   by 1-inch width.
   Lay one cheese strip down the center of biscuit.
   Wrap biscuit around cheese slice. Pinch dough
   at seam to seal seam closed.
   Press top of bread stick into Parmesan cheese.

♥ Place bread sticks on prepared cookie sheet, Parmesan
  cheese side up. If desired, sprinkle lightly with garlic salt.

♥ Bake at 425 degrees for 7 minutes or until tops are light
  golden brown.

Yield: 10 bread sticks

Calories: 69
Percent Fat Calories: 20%
Carbohydrate: 10 grams
Protein: 3 grams

Total Fat: 2 grams
Cholesterol: 2 mg
Dietary Fiber: 0 grams
Sodium: 270 mg

Menu Ideas: Any Italian meal.

Budget
Friendly

Recipe

Parmesan Biscuits

Excellent!

2 tablespoons Butter Bud Sprinkles - dry (found in spice or diet section of grocery store)

¼ cup finely shredded Parmesan cheese

½ teaspoon Italian seasoning (found in spice section)

Non-fat cooking spray

1 (7.5-ounce) can Pillsbury buttermilk biscuits

♥ Preheat oven to 425 degrees.

♥ Spray a cookie sheet with non-fat cooking spray.

♥ Mix Butter Buds, cheese and Italian seasoning together in a 1-gallon zip-lock bag.

♥ Spray both sides of biscuits lightly with non-fat cooking spray.

♥ Put biscuits in bag and shake gently until biscuits are coated with mixture.

♥ Place on prepared cookie sheet.

♥ Sprinkle remaining crumb mixture on top of biscuits.

♥ Bake on the top shelf of oven at 425 degrees for 8 minutes or until golden brown.

Yield: 10 biscuits

Calories: 66
Percent Fat Calories: 20%
Carbohydrate: 11 grams
Protein: 3 grams

Total Fat: 2 grams
Cholesterol: 2 mg
Dietary Fiber: 0 grams
Sodium: 284 mg

Menu Ideas: Any dinner, especially Italian foods, such as lasagna or spaghetti.

Total Time: 15 minutes.

Mushroom Pinwheel Biscuits

Budget Friendly Recipe

*These are extra special, for
extra special meals.*

Beverages, Appetizers & Breads
Great Beginnings

1   (10-ounce) can prepared
    pizza dough (Pillsbury)
½ cup finely shredded
    Parmesan cheese

¾ cup finely chopped fresh
   mushrooms
1 tablespoon dried parsley

♥ Preheat oven to 425 degrees.

♥ Spray an 11x17-inch cookie sheet with non-fat cooking spray.

♥ Roll pizza dough out and press dough with hands to edges
  of prepared cookie sheet.

♥ Sprinkle cheese, mushrooms and parsley over dough.

♥ Roll up jelly-roll style (starting on the long side). Pinch dough
  at edge to seal seam.

♥ With a very sharp knife carefully cut into 12 slices.

♥ Carefully place pinwheels on prepared cookie sheet with each
  biscuit laying flat on its side, so you can see the pinwheel on
  top. Arrange pinwheels as you would when baking a dozen
  cookies, so that sides do not touch.

♥ Bake at 425 degrees for 8 minutes or until tops are golden
  brown.

Yield: 12 biscuits

Calories: 74
Percent Fat Calories: 24%
Carbohydrate: 10 grams
Protein: 4 grams

Total Fat: 2 grams
Cholesterol: 3 mg
Dietary Fiber: 0 grams
Sodium: 198 mg

Menu idea: Any special meal.

Budget
Friendly

Recipe

BACON BISCUITS

The light, smoky flavor of these yummy
biscuits are good for breakfast, brunch or dinner.

2 cups reduced-fat
   Bisquick baking mix
½ cup skim milk
¼ cup applesauce
2 egg whites

1 cup finely shredded
   fat-free cheddar cheese
   (I use Kraft)
1 (3-ounce) jar real bacon
   bits (I use Hormel)

♥ Preheat oven to 375 degrees.

♥ Spray a cookie sheet with non-fat cooking spray.

♥ Mix all ingredients together until well blended.

♥ Drop by rounded tablespoonfuls onto prepared cookie sheet.

♥ Bake for 10 to 12 minutes or until golden brown.

Yield: 24 biscuits

Calories: 62
Percent Fat Calories: 19%
Carbohydrate: 8 grams
Protein: 4 grams

Total Fat: 1 gram
Cholesterol: 3 mg
Dietary Fiber: 0 grams
Sodium: 273 mg

Menu Ideas: Tastes good with any entrée.

PARMESAN GARLIC BISCUITS

Crunchy with a light garlic flavor.

1 (7.5-ounce) can Pillsbury buttermilk biscuits

1 tablespoon Butter Buds Sprinkles - dry

1 teaspoon minced garlic

2 tablespoons finely grated Parmesan cheese

♥ Preheat oven to 425 degrees.

♥ Spray a cookie sheet with non-fat cooking spray.

♥ Sprinkle individual biscuits with Butter Buds Sprinkles.

♥ Spread garlic over tops of biscuits, then lightly sprinkle each biscuit with Parmesan cheese.

♥ Bake in 425 oven for 8 minutes or until golden brown.

Yield: 10 servings

Calories: 59
Percent Fat Calories: 18%
Carbohydrate: 10 grams
Protein: 2 grams

Total Fat: 1 gram
Cholesterol: 1 mg
Dietary Fiber: 0 grams
Sodium: 225 mg

Menu Ideas: *Good with any Italian or homestyle entrée.*

Budget
Friendly

Recipe

BAGEL CHIPS

*This wonderful and easy snack was sent
in by Carolyn Henderson of Howell, Michigan. Wait until
you try this one. You will want to make more than one!*

1   onion or garlic bagel
Non-fat butter-flavored
cooking spray

1   teaspoon Italian
seasoning
¼ teaspoon garlic salt

♥ Preheat oven to 350 degrees.

♥ Spray a cookie sheet with non-fat cooking spray.

♥ With a serrated knife, slice bagel vertically into thin slices.

♥ Arrange on cookie sheet and spray lightly with butter-
flavored cooking spray.

♥ Sprinkle with Italian seasoning and garlic salt.

♥ Bake at 350 degrees for 12 minutes or until crispy.

Yield: 2 servings

Calories: 153
Percent Fat Calories: 5%
Carbohydrate: 30 grams
Protein: 6 grams

Total Fat: 1 gram
Cholesterol: 0 mg
Dietary Fiber: 1 gram
Sodium: 520 mg

**Menu Ideas: *Goes good with
Greek Pasta Salad (page 73) or any fresh,
tossed garden salad.***

*When it comes to our bodies . . .
better a broken bone than
a broken heart.*

SHRIMP SPREAD

*Definitely for extra special occasions.
More special than just shrimp over cocktail sauce
and cream cheese. As pretty as it is yummy!*

1½ cups shredded fat-free
    mozzarella cheese
    (I use Kraft) - divided
1 (8-ounce) package
    fat-free cream cheese
1 (8-ounce) container
    fat-free sour cream

½ cup plus 1 tablespoon
    chopped fresh chives -
    divided
1 (8-ounce) jar cocktail
    sauce
1 pound cooked cocktail
    shrimp (40/50 count) -
    remove tails
½ cup finely chopped tomato

♥ Mix 1 cup of the mozzarella cheese with the cream cheese, sour cream and ½ cup fresh chives until smooth.

♥ Spread on a cake plate.

♥ Cover with cocktail sauce.

♥ Top with remaining ½ cup mozzarella cheese, shrimp, remaining 1 tablespoon chives and tomatoes.

Yield: 16 (3-ounce) servings

Calories: 90	Total Fat: trace
Percent Fat Calories: 5%	Cholesterol: 59 mg
Carbohydrate: 8 grams	Dietary Fiber: 0 grams
Protein: 13 grams	Sodium: 420 mg

Menu Ideas: Serve with crackers.

Seafood Spread: Make exactly the same as the Shrimp Spread recipe but use 8 ounces cooked crab and 8 ounces cooked shrimp.

Yield: 16 (3-ounce) servings

Calories: 95	Total Fat: 1 gram
Percent Fat Calories: 12%	Cholesterol: 44 mg
Carbohydrate: 8 grams	Dietary Fiber: 0 grams
Protein: 12 grams	Sodium: 465 mg

RANCH STACKS

*A versatile appetizer that is
satisfying enough to substitute in place of
a sandwich for packed lunches.*

1 (8-ounce) package fat-free cream cheese - softened
1 cup fat-free sour cream
1 (1-ounce) package Hidden Valley Ranch dip mix - dry
½ cup finely chopped celery
¼ cup finely chopped green onion
9 fat-free flour tortillas

♥ With a mixer on medium speed, beat cream cheese, sour cream and dry Hidden Valley Ranch dip mix together until well mixed.

♥ With a spoon, stir in celery and green onions.

♥ Divide mixture among six individual flour tortillas.

♥ Put one tortilla spread with mixture on top of another tortilla spread with mixture.

♥ Place a third tortilla (which has not been spread with mixture) on top.

♥ You will have 3 tortilla stacks, each 3 layers high.

♥ Press stacks firmly down with hands to secure together.

♥ Cut each stack into 6 pieces.

Yield: 18 (1-wedge) servings

Calories: 87
Percent Fat Calories: 0%
Carbohydrate: 17 grams
Protein: 4 grams

Total Fat: 0 grams
Cholesterol: 2 mg
Dietary Fiber: 1 gram
Sodium: 429 mg

Menu Ideas: Appetizers or lunch.

MUSHROOM BISCUITS

A step above a traditional biscuit.

Budget
Friendly

Recipe

1 (7.5-ounce) can Pillsbury
 biscuits
1 teaspoon minced garlic
 (I use the kind in a jar)
1 teaspoon dried parsley
⅓ cup fat-free cottage
 cheese

¼ cup sliced fresh
 mushrooms
⅛ teaspoon light salt
2 tablespoons fat-free
 Parmesan cheese

♥ Preheat oven to 425 degrees.

♥ Spray an 11x17-inch jelly-roll pan with non-fat cooking spray.

♥ Place biscuits on prepared pan. Set aside.

♥ In a medium bowl, mix garlic, parsley and cottage cheese together with a spoon until smooth and creamy.

♥ Spread mixture over tops of biscuits.

♥ Top each biscuit with two slices of fresh sliced mushrooms.

♥ Sprinkle biscuits with fat-free Parmesan cheese.

♥ Bake at 425 degrees for 10 minutes.

Yield: 10 biscuits

Calories: 60
Percent Fat Calories: 12%
Carbohydrate: 10 grams
Protein: 3 grams

Total Fat: 1 gram
Cholesterol: 1 mg
Dietary Fiber: 0 grams
Sodium: 223 mg

Menu Ideas: Great with any Italian dish.

CRANBERRY CORN MUFFINS

*Good for anytime of the day;
breakfast, snack, lunch or dinner.*

1 (8.5-ounce) package Jiffy
   Corn Muffin mix - dry - do
   not make as directed on box
⅓ cup water

2 egg whites
⅓ cup cheddar cheese
⅓ cup dried cranberries -
   chopped

♥ Preheat oven to 350 degrees.

♥ Spray muffin tins with non-fat cooking spray.

♥ Mix Jiffy mix, water and egg whites. Batter will be lumpy.

♥ Stir in cheese and chopped cranberries.

♥ Fill muffin cups half full.

♥ Bake 15 to 17 minutes or until golden brown.

Yield: 10 muffins

Calories: 133
Percent Fat Calories: 29%
Carbohydrate: 20 grams
Protein: 3 grams

Total Fat: 4 grams
Cholesterol: 4 mg
Dietary Fiber: 2 grams
Sodium: 302 mg

***Menu Ideas: Yummy with a turkey dinner or
Pork Tenderloin (page 250).***

CANDY CANE BISCUITS

*Budget
Friendly*

Recipe

*These cherry biscuits shaped like
candy canes are festive for Christmas meals.*

1 (7.5-ounce) can
    buttermilk biscuits
    (I use Pillsbury)
15 maraschino cherries -
    finely chopped

1 tablespoon Snackwell's
    vanilla frosting
2 tablespoons sugar
2 drops red food coloring

♥ Preheat oven to 425 degrees.

♥ Spray a cookie sheet with non-fat cooking spray.

♥ Press the chopped cherries into each biscuit individually.

♥ Twist and roll each biscuit with hands into a rope.

♥ Shape the ropes into individual candy canes.

♥ Bake for 8 minutes or until bottoms are golden brown.

♥ Microwave frosting for 10 seconds or until hot and bubbly.
   Drizzle frosting over warm candy cane biscuits.

♥ Mix sugar with red food coloring.

♥ Sprinkle sugar on top of canes.

Yield: 10 biscuits

Calories: 82
Percent Fat Calories: 11%
Carbohydrate: 16 grams
Protein: 1 gram

Total Fat: 1 gram
Cholesterol: 0 mg
Dietary Fiber: 0 grams
Sodium: 168 mg

Menu Ideas: Breakfast or brunch.

RAISIN BRAN MUFFINS

*Great to keep on hand for those
"on the go, rushed mornings" when sitting
down for breakfast isn't an option.*

1¼ cups all-purpose flour	1¼ cups raisin bran cereal
1 tablespoon baking powder	1 cup skim milk
⅓ cup packed dark brown sugar	2 egg whites
	¼ cup applesauce

♥ Preheat oven to 400 degrees.

♥ Spray 12 muffin tins with non-fat cooking spray.

♥ Mix flour, baking powder and sugar. Set aside.

♥ In a large bowl, let cereal sit in the milk for 2 minutes.

♥ Stir egg whites and applesauce into soggy cereal until well mixed.

♥ Stir in dry ingredients just until well blended.

♥ Spoon into prepared muffin tins.

♥ Bake at 400 degrees for 20 minutes or until golden brown.

Yield: 12 muffins

Calories: 101	Total Fat: 0 grams
Percent Fat Calories: 0%	Cholesterol: 0 mg
Carbohydrate: 22 grams	Dietary Fiber: 1 gram
Protein: 3 grams	Sodium: 182 mg

Menu Ideas: Breakfast, Brunch buffets or a snack.

Notes

_____
_____
_____
_____
_____
_____
_____
_____
_____
_____
_____
_____
_____
_____
_____
_____
_____
_____
_____
_____
_____
_____
_____

Super Easy Soups & Salads

TABBOULEH TOSSED SALAD

Budget Friendly Recipe

Oh Baby! Is this good!!

1 (1-pound) bag cut-up salad greens (or 1 medium head of iceberg lettuce cut into bite-size pieces)

½ (7-ounce) container tabbouleh (3½ ounces used)

⅓ cup fat-free Red Wine Vinaigrette Salad Dressing (I use Wish-Bone)

½ cup fat-free garlic croutons

♥ Toss everything together except for croutons.

♥ Chill before serving. When ready to eat, top salad with croutons. (Croutons will become soggy if tossed with dressing too long before eating.)

Yield: 4 servings

Calories: 128
Percent Fat Calories: 6%
Carbohydrate: 26 grams
Protein: 5 grams

Total Fat: 1 gram
Cholesterol: 0 mg
Dietary Fiber: 4 grams
Sodium: 324 mg

Budget
Friendly
Recipe

TOMATO BISQUE (SOUP)

This recipe was created by Ted Eagle of Wall, PA. His wife, Oleen, runs one of the nicest television stations I've ever worked with. (Cornerstone TeleVision) This recipe is a step above the traditional tomato soup. . .and it's quite tasty and simple.

1 (26-ounce) can condensed tomato soup (Campbell's)
13 ounces water (½ of soup can)

1 (14.5-ounce) can no-salt-added diced tomatoes (or 3 plum tomatoes, skinned and chopped)
1 cup fat-free half & half (I use Land O Lakes)

♥ Put all ingredients in a big soup pan. Bring to a low boil, stirring constantly until well blended.

♥ Serve hot.

Yield: 7 (1-cup) servings

Calories: 102
Percent Fat Calories: 0%
Carbohydrate: 22 grams
Protein: 5 grams

Total Fat: 0 grams
Cholesterol: 0 mg
Dietary Fiber: 2 grams
Sodium: 660 mg

Menu Ideas: Grilled cheese (low-fat of course).

Super Easy
Soups & Salads

BROCCOLI AND CAULIFLOWER SALAD

Light, sweet and tangy.

Budget Friendly Recipe

2 pounds frozen broccoli and cauliflower - thawed

¼ cup chopped dried cranberries or dried cherries

1 (3-ounce) jar real bacon bits

½ cup T. Marzetti's fat-free Cole Slaw Salad Dressing

♥ Mix all ingredients together until well blended.

♥ Serve chilled.

Yield: 14 (½-cup) servings

Calories: 57
Percent Fat Calories: 20%
Carbohydrate: 8 grams
Protein: 4 grams

Total Fat: 1 gram
Cholesterol: 9 mg
Dietary Fiber: 2 grams
Sodium: 322 mg

Menu Ideas: *Good for anytime of the year. Especially good for summertime meals.*

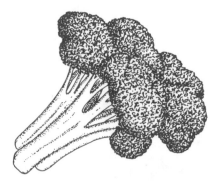

Budget
Friendly
Recipe

PEAS, CHEESE AND
BACON SALAD

Tasty for any picnic, potluck or buffet.

¼ cup T. Marzetti's fat-free
  Cole Slaw Salad Dressing
¼ cup Kraft Free non-fat
  mayonnaise
2 teaspoons sugar
  (or 2 teaspoons Equal
  Spoonful)

1 (1-pound) bag frozen
  green peas
½ cup fat-free shredded
  cheddar cheese
  (I use Kraft)
¼ cup real bacon bits
  (I use Hormel)

♥ In a medium serving bowl, mix salad dressing,
  mayonnaise and sugar (or Equal Spoonful)
  together briskly until well mixed.

♥ Stir in peas, cheese and bacon.

♥ Serve chilled.

**Note: If peas have frozen ice crystals on them, put peas in
a strainer and run under cold water until ice is dissolved.**

Yield: 7 (½-cup) servings

With Sugar:
Calories: 100
Percent Fat Calories: 9%
Carbohydrate: 15 grams
Protein: 8 grams

Total Fat: 1 gram
Cholesterol: 8 mg
Dietary Fiber: 3 grams
Sodium: 435 mg

With Equal:
Calories: 95
Percent Fat Calories: 9%
Carbohydrate: 14 grams
Protein: 8 grams

Total Fat: 1 gram
Cholesterol: 8 mg
Dietary Fiber: 3 grams
Sodium: 435 mg

Menu Ideas: Will accompany any summer meal.

Super Easy
Soups & Salads

BUTTERMILK RANCH SALAD DRESSING

Budget Friendly Recipe

This puts other fat-free Ranch salad dressings to shame. It is so good!

1 (0.59-ounce) envelope fat-free Hidden Valley Original Ranch dip mix - dry (do not make as directed on envelope)

1 cup fat-free sour cream (I use Breakstone)
1 cup low-fat buttermilk

♥ Mix all ingredients until well blended.
♥ Serve chilled.

Yield: 16 (2-tablespoon) servings

Calories: 27
Percent Fat Calories: 0%
Carbohydrate: 4 grams
Protein: 2 grams

Total Fat: 0 grams
Cholesterol: 2 mg
Dietary Fiber: 0 grams
Sodium: 151 mg

Menu Ideas: Great on fresh salad greens. Also good as a dip with fresh vegetables.

Buttermilk-Dill Salad Dressing: Make exactly as Buttermilk Ranch Salad Dressing, but also stir in 1 teaspoon dried dill. Serve chilled.

Yield: 16 (2-tablespoon) servings

Calories: 27
Percent Fat Calories: 0%
Carbohydrate: 4 grams
Protein: 2 grams

Total Fat: 0 grams
Cholesterol: 2 mg
Dietary Fiber: 0 grams
Sodium: 151 mg

Super Easy Soups & Salads

Budget
Friendly
Recipe

SWEET AND SOUR
BACON SALAD DRESSING

*What? Bacon salad dressing that's low-fat?
Hard to believe isn't it? If you like sweet
and sour, you're gonna love this!*

½ cup Equal Spoonful
   (or ½ cup sugar)
¼ cup apple cider vinegar
¼ cup skim milk

⅔ cup fat-free sour cream
½ (3-ounce) jar real bacon
   bits (I use Hormel -
   Note: only use ½ of the
   3-ounce jar!!)

**Super Easy
Soups & Salads**

♥ With a whisk, briskly stir together all ingredients until well blended.

♥ Keep chilled until ready to serve.

Yield: 12 (2-tablespoon) servings

With Equal Spoonful:

Calories: 33
Percent Fat Calories: 21%
Carbohydrate: 3 grams
Protein: 2 grams

Total Fat: 1 gram
Cholesterol: 4 mg
Dietary Fiber: 0 grams
Sodium: 128 mg

With Sugar:

Calories: 62
Percent Fat Calories: 10%
Carbohydrate: 11 grams
Protein: 2 grams

Total Fat: 1 gram
Cholesterol: 4 mg
Dietary Fiber: 0 grams
Sodium: 128 mg

**Menu Ideas: Absolutely delicious on fresh
salad greens. It tastes terrific on any type of lettuce.**

Total Time: 10 minutes.

REUBEN SALAD

If you like Reuben sandwiches you'll like this!

5 cups chopped iceberg lettuce (or 1 [10-ounce] bag cut-up lettuce)

1 (14-ounce) can sauerkraut - rinsed and squeezed dry with hands

2 slices fat-free Swiss cheese - cut into pieces (I use Kraft)

1 (2.5-ounce) package lean, thin sliced corned beef (found next to chipped beef in refrigerator section)

½ cup fat-free Thousand Island salad dressing

½ cup rye croutons (fat-free are available)

♥ Toss all ingredients together with dressing.

♥ Serve immediately.

Note: Do not toss with dressing until its time to eat. Otherwise salad will get soggy.

Yield: 5 (1-cup) servings

Calories: 87
Percent Fat Calories: 13%
Carbohydrate: 14 grams
Protein: 5 grams

Total Fat: 1 gram
Cholesterol: 10 mg
Dietary Fiber: 3 grams
Sodium: 957 mg

Menu Ideas: Grilled chicken or fish entrées.

Living happily married (as their parents) is one of the best gifts we can give our children.

Budget Friendly Recipe

HONEY MUSTARD TURKEY SALAD

A wonderful way to use leftover turkey after the holidays!

2 tablespoons honey
½ cup Miracle Whip Light
½ cup Miracle Whip Free
¼ cup mustard

4 cups cubed cooked turkey breast
½ cup chopped celery
10 red grapes - each cut into ¼-inch slices

♥ Mix honey, Miracle Whip Light, Miracle Whip Free and mustard together until well mixed.

♥ Stir in remaining ingredients until well blended.

Note: After mixing the dressing with the turkey, the mixture will stir down to approximately 3 cups.

Yield: 6 (½-cup) servings

Calories: 239
Percent Fat Calories: 21%
Carbohydrate: 16 grams
Protein: 29 grams

Total Fat: 5 grams
Cholesterol: 78 mg
Dietary Fiber: 0 grams
Sodium: 509 mg

Menu Ideas: As a sandwich between toast with iceberg lettuce. By itself with melon and fresh fruit, or on top of a bed of salad greens.

Honey Mustard Chicken Salad: Substitute chicken breast for the turkey.

Yield: 6 (½-cup) servings

Calories: 265
Percent Fat Calories: 28%
Carbohydrate: 16 grams
Protein: 30 grams

Total Fat: 8 grams
Cholesterol: 79 mg
Dietary Fiber: 0 grams
Sodium: 529 mg

Super Easy Soups & Salads

GREEK SALAD

*Greek condiments turn boring
tossed salad into something special.*

¼ teaspoon dried oregano - crushed

1 (14.5-ounce) can no-salt-added diced tomatoes - drained (or 18 cherry tomatoes)

1 cup fat-free Red Wine Vinegar Salad Dressing (I use Kraft)

2 (10-ounce) bags cut lettuce (I use Dole - European Brand, or if you'd like, you can cut up a combination totaling 14 cups of iceberg lettuce and curly endive)

½ cup chopped onion (approximately one small onion)

12 small, pitted black olives - cut into thin slices

¼ cup finely crumbled feta cheese (approximately 1½ ounces)

♥ In a small bowl, mix together dried oregano, diced tomatoes and salad dressing until well mixed. Set aside and keep refrigerated until ready to eat.

♥ In a large serving bowl, toss lettuce and chopped onion together. Keep chilled until ready to serve.

♥ Just before serving, toss salad with salad dressing mixture until well coated.

♥ Top with olives and sprinkle with finely crumbled feta cheese.

♥ Serve chilled.

Note: Do not toss with salad dressing until ready to serve, as this will make your salad soggy.

Super Easy
Soups & Salads

(Greek Salad continued)

Yield: 7 (2-cup) servings

Calories: 60
Percent Fat Calories: 29%
Carbohydrate: 9 grams
Protein: 2 grams

Total Fat: 2 grams
Cholesterol: 5 mg
Dietary Fiber: 2 grams
Sodium: 577 mg

Menu Ideas: Accompanies omelets wonderfully for brunches! Also delicious with Italian entrées. Great with baked or grilled lean meats, chicken or fish.

Total Time: 10 minutes or less.

Budget
Friendly

Recipe

SLAW SALAD

A tangy and tart salad that makes a wonderful alternative for cole slaw.

½ cup Marzetti's fat-free Cole Slaw Salad Dressing
¼ cup sweetened dried cranberries (I use Ocean Spray)

1 (1-pound) bag gourmet lettuce mixture (iceberg, romaine, escarole, endive, radicchio)
1 medium Gala apple (or Red Delicious) - chopped

♥ Mix all ingredients together.
♥ Serve chilled.

Yield: 5 (1½-cup) servings

Calories: 89
Percent Fat Calories: 0%
Carbohydrate: 21 grams
Protein: 2 grams

Total Fat: 0 grams
Cholesterol: 12 mg
Dietary Fiber: 3 grams
Sodium: 335 mg

Menu Ideas: Goes good with (Oven) Fried Catfish (page 145).

CHERRY HOLIDAY SALAD

Great for the holidays with turkey or ham. Slightly tart and tangy.

1 cup diet 7-Up or diet Sprite

1 (.35-ounce) package sugar-free cherry gelatin - dry - do not make as directed on box (I use Royal)

1 (14.5-ounce) can pitted, tart, red cherries in water (I use Thank You Brand)

1 (11-ounce) can mandarin oranges

¼ cup Equal Spoonful sweetener (or ¼ cup sugar)

1 (8-ounce) container Cool Whip Free

¼ cup finely chopped walnuts

♥ Heat 7-Up in microwave on high for one minute.

♥ In a large bowl, briskly stir gelatin into hot 7-Up. Stir until completely dissolved.

♥ Drain juices from cherries and oranges into gelatin. Stir until well mixed.

♥ On a dinner plate, smash cherries with a potato masher.

♥ Add sweetener to smashed cherries and stir until well mixed.

♥ With a whisk, briskly stir sweetened cherries, oranges, Cool Whip Free and chopped walnuts into gelatin until well mixed.

♥ Pour into a pretty serving bowl (preferably glass so you can see the pretty layers)

♥ Refrigerate until firm. (I like to make the night or morning before needed.)

(Cherry Holiday Salad continued)

Yield: 10 servings

<u>With Equal Spoonful:</u>

Calories: 88

Percent Fat Calories: 21%

Carbohydrate: 15 grams

Protein: 1 gram

Total Fat: 2 grams

Cholesterol: 0 mg

Dietary Fiber: 1 gram

Sodium: 46 mg

<u>With Sugar:</u>

Calories: 106

Percent Fat Calories: 17%

Carbohydrate: 20 grams

Protein: 1 gram

Total Fat: 2 grams

Cholesterol: 0 mg

Dietary Fiber: 1 gram

Sodium: 46 mg

Menu Ideas: Great for potlucks, buffets or holiday meals.

Super Easy
Soups & Salads

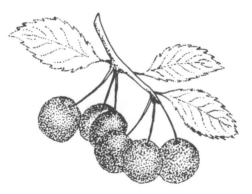

SPINACH ORANGE SALAD

Pretty and light, the combination is just right!

Budget Friendly Recipe

1 (10-ounce) package fresh spinach - stems removed if desired
1 (11-ounce) can mandarin oranges
¼ cup real bacon bits (I use Hormel - about ⅓ jar)

½ cup fat-free sour cream (I use Breakstone)
2 tablespoons sugar (or Equal Spoonful)
½ cup fat-free croutons
¼ medium-sized red onion - cut into ⅛-inch rings and separated

♥ Put spinach in a large bowl. Set aside.

♥ Drain the juice from the mandarin oranges into another bowl. Set oranges in can aside.

♥ With a whisk, briskly mix the drained mandarin juice, bacon bits, fat-free sour cream and sugar until well blended.

♥ Toss spinach with dressing. Garnish salad with orange segments, croutons and onions.

Note: Do not toss salad or croutons in dressing until ready to serve, or salad will become soggy.

Yield: 8 (1-cup) side salads or 4 (2-cups) entrée salads

With Sugar: (8 servings)

Calories: 69
Percent Fat Calories: 10%
Carbohydrate: 12 grams
Protein: 4 grams

Total Fat: 1 gram
Cholesterol: 4 mg
Dietary Fiber: 1 gram
Sodium: 165 mg

With Equal Spoonful: (8 servings)

Calories: 58
Percent Fat Calories: 12%
Carbohydrate: 9 grams
Protein: 4 grams

Total Fat: 1 gram
Cholesterol: 4 mg
Dietary Fiber: 1 gram
Sodium: 165 mg

Menu Ideas: As an entrée serve with Bagel Chips (page 39) and Maraschino Chocolate Cherry Cream Pie for dessert (page 261 of "Busy People's Low-Fat Cookbook").

As a side salad it is delicious with any lean grilled meat.

ASPARAGUS SALAD

A taste of Spring!!

1   pound fresh asparagus
¾ cup fat-free Red Wine
    Vinegar Salad Dressing

1   teaspoon sugar (or Equal
    Spoonful)

♥ Cook asparagus in boiling water for 5 minutes. Drain.

♥ Gently toss asparagus with dressing and sugar.

Yield: 5 (½-cup) servings

*Super Easy
Soups & Salads*

With Sugar:

Calories: 42
Percent Fat Calories: 0%
Carbohydrate: 9 grams
Protein: 2 grams

Total Fat: 0 grams
Cholesterol: 0 mg
Dietary Fiber: 2 grams
Sodium: 482 mg

With Equal:

Calories: 39
Percent Fat Calories: 0%
Carbohydrate: 8 grams
Protein: 2 grams

Total Fat: 0 grams
Cholesterol: 0 mg
Dietary Fiber: 2 grams
Sodium: 482 mg

Menu Ideas: Accompanies any lean grilled meat.

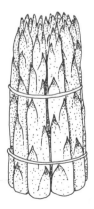

Total Time: 15 minutes.

UNSTUFFED
GREEN PEPPER SOUP

Budget Friendly Recipe

If you like stuffed green peppers, you'll like this!

½ pound ground beef eye of round

3 cups Health Valley fat-free, no-salt-added beef broth (or made with bouillon)

2 cups low-sodium V8 juice (or three 5.5-ounce cans)

2 (14.5-ounce) cans no-salt-added stewed tomatoes

1 cup frozen or fresh chopped green peppers

1 cup frozen or fresh chopped onion

1 cup instant rice

Super Easy
Soups & Salads

Stove top Method:

♥ Bring everything, except rice, to a boil over high heat in a large, nonstick soup pan.

♥ Let boil 2 minutes, stirring occasionally.

♥ Turn off heat. Stir in rice. Cover and let sit for 5 minutes.

♥ Serve hot.

♥ If desired, season with ground black pepper to taste.

Crockpot Method:

♥ Put all ingredients, except rice, in a large crockpot.

♥ Stir until well mixed. Cover.

♥ Cook on low for 8 to 10 hours or on high for 4 to 5 hours.

♥ Before serving, stir in rice. Cover and let sit 5 minutes.

♥ Serve hot.

Yield: 8 (1-cup) servings

Calories: 144
Percent Fat Calories: 8%
Carbohydrate: 21 grams
Protein: 11 grams

Total Fat: 1 gram
Cholesterol: 15 mg
Dietary Fiber: 3 grams
Sodium: 92 mg

Menu Ideas: Sourdough or French bread.

Budget
Friendly

Recipe

HEN AND EGGS TOSSED SALAD

Best served with
Bacon Salad Dressing (page 53). Delicious!

8 ounces cooked chicken breast - cut into tiny pieces

8 cups or 1 (1-pound) bag of Dole cut-up lettuce (I like romaine and iceberg for this salad)

½ cup Egg Beaters - cooked* (like scrambled eggs but with nothing added) and chilled

½ cup fat-free Parmesan- or garlic-flavored croutons

♥ Toss all ingredients together except croutons.

♥ Add croutons and serve.

*Note: To prepare eggs quickly, cook in microwave for 1 minute 30 seconds. Scramble with a whisk after cooking. Put in freezer for 2 to 3 minutes to chill.

Note: Do not add dressing or croutons until ready to serve or the salad will get soggy!

Yield: 8 (1-cup) side servings

Calories: 65
Percent Fat Calories: 16%
Carbohydrate: 2 grams
Protein: 11 grams

Total Fat: 1 gram
Cholesterol: 24 mg
Dietary Fiber: 1 gram
Sodium: 61 mg

Yield: 4 (2-cup) entrée size servings

Calories: 129
Percent Fat Calories: 16%
Carbohydrate: 4 grams
Protein: 22 grams

Total Fat: 2 grams
Cholesterol: 48 mg
Dietary Fiber: 2 grams
Sodium: 122 mg

Menu Ideas: Great as a meal in itself for lunch. Also good for buffets and potlucks.

Super Easy
Soups & Salads

Total Time: 25 minutes or less, including 10 minutes to cut meat.

World's
Easiest Vegetable Soup

Budget
Friendly

Recipe

Nothin' like a hot bowl of soup on a cold wintry day.

1   (46-ounce) can V8
    vegetable juice
4   cups Health Valley fat-
    free, no-salt-added beef
    broth (or made from beef
    bouillon)

4   (15.25-ounce) cans mixed
    vegetables - drained
1   teaspoon salad
    seasoning spices
    (I use Durkee - found in
    seasoning aisle)

Stove top Method:

♥ Bring all ingredients to a boil over high heat in a large, nonstick soup pan.

♥ If desired mash soup in pot for a few minutes by hand with a potato masher to make soup a little thicker. Serve hot.

Crockpot Method:

♥ Mix all ingredients in a 6-quart or larger crockpot.

♥ Cook on low for 4 hours or on high for 2 hours.

Yield: 16 (1-cup) servings

Calories: 60
Percent Fat Calories: 0%
Carbohydrate: 11 grams
Protein: 4 grams

Total Fat: 0 grams
Cholesterol: 0 mg
Dietary Fiber: 3 grams
Sodium: 375 mg

Total Time: 15 minutes or less.

Beef Vegetable Soup: Make exactly as World's Easiest Vegetable Soup and add 2 pounds of eye of round, cut into tiny bite-size pieces, with other ingredients at beginning of recipe. (No need to pre-cook. The meat will cook while boiling).

(World's Easiest Vegetable Soup continued)

Yield: 20 (1-cup) servings

Calories: 108
Percent Fat Calories: 18%
Carbohydrate: 9 grams
Protein: 13 grams

Total Fat: 2 grams
Cholesterol: 24 mg
Dietary Fiber: 2 grams
Sodium: 324 mg

***Menu Ideas: Grilled Cheese Sandwiches
(page 34 of "Busy People's Low-Fat Cookbook") and
Orange Sugar Cookies (page 172 of this book).***

Total Time: 15 minutes or less.

MUSHROOM CHOWDER

Budget
Friendly
Recipe

*This thick, creamy, buttery comfort food
makes you feel warm and good inside with every bite!*

Super Easy
Soups & Salads

8 cups water
8 chicken bouillon cubes
1 tablespoon minced garlic
(I use the kind in the jar)
2 packets of Butter Buds -
dry (or 2 tablespoons
Butter Bud Sprinkles)

1½ pounds fresh mushrooms
- sliced
4 ounces cooked, smoked,
lean ham - chopped
3 (2-ounce) packages
instant mashed
potatoes (I use Martha
White spud flakes)

♥ Put everything except instant mashed potatoes in a large
soup pot. Cover. Turn heat on high and cook for 10 minutes.

♥ Stir in the instant mashed potatoes, one packet at a time.
Serve immediately.

Yield: 10 (1-cup) servings

Calories: 109
Percent Fat Calories: 10%
Carbohydrate: 19 grams
Protein: 6 grams

Total Fat: 1 gram
Cholesterol: 7 mg
Dietary Fiber: 2 grams
Sodium: 1163 mg

Menu Ideas: Saltine crackers and tossed salad.

Budget
Friendly

Recipe

DELUXE BEAN SOUP

This savory, thick, hearty soup is a winner.

2 (48-ounce) jars Randall's deluxe beans

8 cups Health Valley fat-free, no-salt-added beef broth (or made from bouillon)

1 cup frozen chopped onions

2 (14-ounce) packages fat-free smoked sausage - cut into ¼-inch pieces - (I use Butterball)

1 (10¾-ounce) can condensed tomato soup

1 teaspoon dried dill

♥ Put beans, beef broth and onions into a large soup pan. Mix well.

♥ Remove 4 cups of beans and broth at a time and puree in a blender until a total of 12 cups has been pureed. Return puree to soup pan.

♥ Turn heat on high. Add smoked sausage, tomato soup and dill. Bring to a boil.

♥ Serve hot.

Yield: 21 (1-cup) servings

Calories: 173
Percent Fat Calories: 3%
Carbohydrate: 27 grams
Protein: 15 grams

Total Fat: 1 gram
Cholesterol: 16 mg
Dietary Fiber: 11 grams
Sodium: 1016 mg

Menu Ideas: Sweet Corn Bread (page 78) and Spiced Apples (page 146, both recipes are in "Busy People's Low-Fat Cookbook").

CREAM OF POTATO SOUP

Satisfying and filling.
Excellent for a cold winter's day!

¼ cup all-purpose flour
1 pint fat-free half & half
  (I use Land O Lakes)
2 cups skim milk
1 pound fat-free hash
  browns
½ cup frozen or fresh
  chopped onion

1 (3-ounce) jar real bacon
  bits (I use Hormel)
  (or ¼ pound chopped
  smoked ham)
½ teaspoon dried dill weed
1 tablespoon Butter Buds
  Sprinkles - dry

♥ In a large, nonstick Dutch oven or soup pot, with a whisk, briskly stir flour into half & half and skim milk.

♥ Once flour is completely dissolved, add remaining ingredients and cook over medium-high heat, stirring frequently.

♥ Once boiling, continue to cook and stir at a full boil for 3 to 5 minutes, or until potatoes are tender. Remove from heat.

♥ If desired, season with lite salt and pepper.

Yield: 5 (1-cup) servings

With bacon bits:
Calories: 263
Percent Fat Calories: 13%
Carbohydrate: 42 grams
Protein: 19 grams

Total Fat: 4 grams
Cholesterol: 14 mg
Dietary Fiber: 2 grams
Sodium: 784 mg

With ham:
Calories: 240
Percent Fat Calories: 7%
Carbohydrate: 41 grams
Protein: 18 grams

Total Fat: 2 grams
Cholesterol: 14 mg
Dietary Fiber: 2 grams
Sodium: 540 mg

Menu Ideas: Tossed salad or fresh vegetable tray and fat-free saltine crackers.

Budget Friendly Recipe

HAM AND YAM SOUP

This reminds me of Split Pea Soup,
but with it's own unique, savory flavor.

8 cups fat-free, reduced-sodium chicken broth (or made from bouillon)

3 medium yams - cut into tiny ¼-inch pieces (about 2 pounds)

¼ cup Butter Buds Sprinkles - dry

1 pound extra lean honey smoked ham - cut into tiny pieces

1¼ cups instant potatoes (I use Betty Crocker Potato Buds) - dry

2 tablespoons packed brown sugar

♥ In a large, nonstick soup pan (or Dutch oven) bring chicken broth, yams, Butter Bud Sprinkles and ham to a full boil. Let boil 3 to 4 minutes, or until yams are tender.

♥ Take 3 cups of the ham and yams from the broth and put into a blender. Add 1 cup of broth to the blender. Cover. Turn the blender on high until pureed. Stir puree back into the pot.

♥ Stir in instant potatoes and sugar until potatoes are dissolved.

♥ Serve hot.

Yield: 10 (1-cup) servings

Calories: 304
Percent Fat Calories: 8%
Carbohydrate: 53 grams
Protein: 17 grams

Total Fat: 3 grams
Cholesterol: 25 mg
Dietary Fiber: 5 grams
Sodium: 1132 mg

Menu Ideas: Pinwheel Dinner Rolls (page 82) and Peaches and Cream Gelatin Salad (page 96, both recipes from "Busy People's Low-Fat Cookbook").

Bar-B-Qued Bean Salad

*A tangy and colorful side salad
that's great for picnics.*

³/₄ cup of your favorite
barbecue sauce

1 tablespoon packed brown
sugar

2 (16-ounce) cans baked
beans - drained

1 cup frozen chopped onion
(or 1 medium chopped)

1 (15.5-ounce) can shoepeg
corn - drained

1 medium sweet red pepper
- chopped

1 (3-ounce) jar real bacon
bits

♥ In microwave, heat barbecue sauce and brown sugar together
for 30 seconds or until brown sugar is completely dissolved.

♥ Put remaining ingredients in a medium serving bowl. Toss
well with barbecue sauce mixture. Eat as is or keep chilled
until ready to serve.

Yield: 10 (½-cup) servings

Calories: 174
Percent Fat Calories: 13%
Carbohydrate: 31 grams
Protein: 9 grams

Total Fat: 3 grams
Cholesterol: 6 mg
Dietary Fiber: 6 grams
Sodium: 878 mg

Menu Ideas: Grilled chicken.

*"The best thing I like to
make for dinner is reservations."*

Liz Torda

Budget
Friendly
Recipe

FRESH FRUIT BREAKFAST SALAD

Perfect for breakfast, instead of fruit juice. The vibrant color combination is beautiful!

1 cup cold water
1 tablespoon lemon juice (from a bottle is fine)
3 medium bananas - cut into ½-inch slices
1 pint fresh strawberries - cut into ⅓-inch slices

4 clementines (or navel oranges) - sliced into ⅓-inch rings, then sections separated
2 packets Equal Sweetener (or 1 tablespoon sugar)

♥ In a medium serving bowl, mix cold water and lemon juice together.

♥ Soak banana slices in lemon-water for 4 minutes.

♥ Drain lemon-water and discard.

♥ Very gently stir sliced strawberries, clementine (or orange) sections and Equal into bananas.

♥ Cover. Keep chilled until ready to eat.

Yield: 10 (½-cup) servings

With Equal:
Calories: 68
Percent Fat Calories: 0%
Carbohydrate: 17 grams
Protein: 1 gram
Total Fat: 0 grams
Cholesterol: 0 mg
Dietary Fiber: 3 grams
Sodium: 1 mg

With Sugar:
Calories: 72
Percent Fat Calories: 0%
Carbohydrate: 18 grams
Protein: 1 gram
Total Fat: 0 grams
Cholesterol: 0 mg
Dietary Fiber: 3 grams
Sodium: 1 mg

Menu Ideas: Great for breakfast, brunch or with fat-free cottage cheese for lunch.

Super Easy Soups & Salads

Total Time: (Stove top): 13 minutes or less (including sitting time).
(Crockpot): 4 to 5 hours on high or 8 to 10 hours on low.

UNSTUFFED CABBAGE SOUP

Budget Friendly Recipe

*If you like stuffed
cabbage rolls, you'll like this!*

1 pound ground beef eye of round

6 cups Health Valley fat-free, no-salt-added beef broth (or made with bouillon)

4 cups low-sodium V8 vegetable juice

2 (14.5-ounce) cans no-salt-added stewed tomatoes

2 cups frozen or fresh chopped onion

1 (1-pound) bag cole slaw mix (or 10 cups shredded fresh green cabbage)

2 cups instant rice

Stove top Method:

♥ Bring everything, except rice, to a boil over high heat in a large, nonstick soup pan.

♥ Let boil 5 minutes, stirring occasionally.

♥ Turn off heat and stir in rice.

♥ Cover and let sit for 5 minutes.

♥ Serve hot.

♥ If desired, season with ground black pepper to taste.

Crockpot Method:

♥ Put all ingredients, except rice, in a large crockpot. Stir well. Cover.

♥ Cook on low for 8 to 10 hours or on high for 4 to 5 hours.

♥ Before serving, stir in rice. Cover and let sit 5 minutes.

♥ Serve hot.

Yield: 16 (1-cup) servings

Calories: 131
Percent Fat Calories: 9%
Carbohydrate: 18 grams
Protein: 11 grams

Total Fat: 1 gram
Cholesterol: 15 mg
Dietary Fiber: 2 grams
Sodium: 91 mg

**Menu Ideas: Serve with French bread and Oreo Mousse
(page 254 of "Busy People's Low-Fat Cookbook").**

Total Time: 20 minutes or less (derived mostly from cutting).

Budget Friendly Recipe

GREEK PASTA SALAD

You would not believe how good this tastes!

16 ounces of your favorite pasta - cooked (for faster preparation, cook extra pasta sometime the week before. Store cooked pasta in cold water and refrigerate. All you have to do is drain water and the pasta is all set.)

1½ cups fat-free Red Wine Vinegar Salad Dressing (I use Kraft)

1 (7-ounce) package tabbouleh (I use Oasis brand, which has 6 grams of fat per 7 ounces)

1 ounce feta cheese - finely crumbled

1 large tomato - cut into ½-inch chunks

12 medium, pitted black olives - slice each into thirds

1 large cucumber - cut into tiny pieces

♥ Mix all ingredients together. Keep chilled until ready to serve.

Yield: 14 (½-cup) servings

Calories: 200
Percent Fat Calories: 8%
Carbohydrate: 39 grams
Protein: 6 grams

Total Fat: 2 grams
Cholesterol: 2 mg
Dietary Fiber: 2 grams
Sodium: 404 mg

Menu Ideas: Cookouts, salad bars and picnics.

TACO CHOWDER

Budget
Friendly

Recipe

Great served on a cold day! It'll warm you from head to toe! A flavorful blend of chili and tacos.

1 pound ground turkey breast

1 (1.25-ounce) packet taco seasoning

1 (28-ounce) can no-salt-added diced tomatoes - do not drain

2 (16-ounce) cans fat-free refried beans (I use Old El Paso)

1 (14.5-ounce) can Health Valley fat-free, no-salt-added beef broth

1 (15-ounce) can light red kidney beans - do not drain

1 (15.25-ounce) can whole kernel golden sweet corn - do not drain

♥ Spray a nonstick soup pan with non-fat cooking spray. Cook meat and taco seasoning over medium heat until fully cooked.

♥ Add diced tomatoes, refried beans, beef broth, kidney beans and corn.

♥ Bring to a boil over high heat. Once it comes to a boil, it's ready to serve.

♥ Serving Ideas: If desired, lightly sprinkle with fat-free cheddar cheese or crushed baked tortilla chips.

Yield: 13 (1-cup servings)

Calories: 172
Percent Fat Calories: 4%
Carbohydrate: 26 grams
Protein: 16 grams

Total Fat: 1 gram
Cholesterol: 24 mg
Dietary Fiber: 7 grams
Sodium: 562 mg

Menu Ideas: Great served with cornbread on the side, or with half of a grilled cheese sandwich.

Budget Friendly Recipe

HOLIDAY FRUIT SALAD

The beautiful colors
give this tasty salad its name.

1 (16-ounce) can jellied whole cranberries
3 cups miniature marshmallows

2 large Gala or Red Delicious apples - unpeeled, cored and chopped
30 seedless green grapes
1 (12-ounce) container Cool Whip Free

♥ Mix all ingredients together until well blended.
♥ Serve chilled.

Yield: 12 (½-cup) servings

Calories: 168
Percent Fat Calories: 0%
Carbohydrate: 40 grams
Protein: 0 grams

Total Fat: 0 grams
Cholesterol: 0 mg
Dietary Fiber: 2 grams
Sodium: 30 mg

Menu Ideas: Good for holiday
get-togethers when serving ham or turkey.

Super Easy Soups & Salads

" The #1 problem with most
people's priorities is that their
#1 priority is themselves."

Tracy Hall

Total Time: (Stove top) 20 minutes or less. (Crockpot) 8 to 9 hours on low or 4 hours on high.

SEAFOOD CHOWDER

An elaborate chowder that is definitely for a special meal!

1 pint fat-free half & half (Land O Lakes)

1 (6-ounce) package frozen small shrimp

2 (6.5-ounce) cans minced clams - do not drain

1 (8-ounce) package imitation scallops (Louis Kemp Seafood Co.)

1 (8-ounce) package imitation crab (Louis Kemp Seafood Co.)

3 (10¾-ounce) cans 98% fat-free Campbell's New England clam chowder

1 pound fat-free frozen hash browns

Stove top Method:

♥ Put everything into a large, nonstick Dutch oven or soup pot.

♥ Cook on medium-high heat, stirring constantly. (So that the bottom won't burn.)

♥ Once boiling, cook and stir an additional 3 to 4 minutes or until potatoes are tender.

♥ If desired, add pepper to taste before serving.

Crockpot Method:

♥ Mix all ingredients in a crockpot until well mixed. Cover. Cook on low for 8 to 9 hours or on high for 4 hours.

♥ If desired, add pepper to taste before serving.

Yield: 10 (1-cup) servings

Calories: 215
Percent Fat Calories: 10%
Carbohydrate: 31 grams
Protein: 19 grams

Total Fat: 2 grams
Cholesterol: 59 mg
Dietary Fiber: 1 gram
Sodium: 1321 mg

Menu Ideas: Tossed salad, fresh vegetables with fat-free dip and fat-free oyster crackers.

Budget
Friendly

Recipe

Pizza Soup

A tasty twist to tomato soup.

1 (14-ounce) jar Ragu pizza sauce (Family Style)
½ cup frozen or fresh chopped onion
1 (4-ounce) can sliced mushrooms - drained
1 ounce thinly sliced pepperoni - cut into tiny strips

1 (26-ounce) can condensed tomato soup (Campbell's)
26 ounces water (use soup can)
1 cup shredded fat-free mozzarella cheese

♥ In a large, nonstick soup pan, bring everything except cheese to a boil over medium-high heat, stirring occasionally.

♥ Once boiling, reduce heat and let simmer for 3 to 4 minutes.

♥ Garnish each serving with mozzarella cheese.

♥ Serve hot.

Yield: 7 (1-cup) servings

Calories: 143
Percent Fat Calories: 15%
Carbohydrate: 21 grams
Protein: 9 grams

Total Fat: 2 grams
Cholesterol: 6 mg
Dietary Fiber: 3 grams
Sodium: 1164 mg

Menu Ideas: Italian Bread Sticks or Garlic Toast (page 79 of "Busy People's Low-Fat Cookbook").

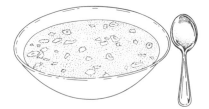

HOT POTATO SALAD

Budget Friendly Recipe

If you like German Potato Salad, you'll like this. It is not sweet. Good for picnics, cookouts, potlucks, etc.

4 large potatoes with skins on (about 2 pounds)
1 tablespoon minced garlic (I use the kind in a jar)
¾ cup fat-free Red Wine Vinegar Salad Dressing
¼ cup fresh chopped chives
1 cup shredded fat-free cheddar cheese (I use Kraft)
1 (3-ounce) jar real bacon bits

♥ Poke holes into potatoes with a fork. Microwave potatoes for about 10 minutes or until fully cooked.

♥ Cut potatoes into bite-size chunks, leaving skins on. Put in freezer for 2 to 3 minutes to cool.

♥ In the meantime, mix garlic, salad dressing and chives together until well blended in large serving bowl.

♥ Gently stir potatoes, cheese and bacon bits into dressing. Serve as is or microwave 3 to 4 minutes.

Yield: 14 (½-cup) servings

Calories: 91
Percent Fat Calories: 12%
Carbohydrate: 14 grams
Protein: 6 grams
Total Fat: 1 gram
Cholesterol: 6 mg
Dietary Fiber: 1 gram
Sodium: 433 mg

Menu Ideas: Good side dish with any lean meat.

Great people are ordinary people with great determination.

Budget
Friendly

Recipe

MINESTRONE SOUP

Hearty and healthy! Just the way we like it!

1 (46-ounce) can tomato juice

1 pound beef eye of round - cut into tiny pieces

1 (14-ounce) jar of your favorite pizza sauce (I use Ragu' Family Style)

3 (15.25-ounce) cans mixed vegetables - do not drain

1 (15-ounce) can red kidney beans - do not drain

2 (14.5-ounce) cans no-salt-added stewed tomatoes - do not drain

2 cups dry elbow macaroni

♥ In a large, nonstick soup pan, bring all ingredients, except macaroni, to a full boil over high heat.

♥ Stir in elbow macaroni. Return to a boil. Cook, uncovered, stirring frequently for 8 minutes.

Yield: 18 (1-cup servings)

Calories: 157
Percent Fat Calories: 10%
Carbohydrate: 25 grams
Protein: 11 grams

Total Fat: 2 grams
Cholesterol: 14 mg
Dietary Fiber: 6 grams
Sodium: 617 mg

Menu Ideas: Garlic Bread or Garlic Toast
(page 79 of "Busy People's Low-Fat Cookbook").

Super Easy Soups & Salads

Total Time: 30 minutes or less.

CHICKEN LEMON SOUP

*Perfect substitution for traditional
chicken noodle soup, especially if you're feeling
under the weather. As grandma would say,
"It's good for what ails you."*

16 cups fat-free, reduced-
sodium chicken broth
(or 16 chicken bouillon
cubes dissolved in 16
cups of water)
2 cups sliced fresh or
frozen carrots (about
4 large carrots)
1½ cups chopped celery
1 pound skinless, boneless
chicken breast - cut into
tiny bite-size pieces

1 medium onion - chopped
(or 1 cup frozen chopped
onion is fine)
1 tablespoon dried parsley
(or 2 tablespoons
chopped fresh)
1 (12-ounce) package
lemon-pepper flavored
penne rigate pasta (I use
Pasta LaBella Brand, but
any lemon-flavored pasta
is fine.)

♥ Put everything into a large soup pot except lemon-pepper
flavored pasta. Cook over high heat, stirring occasionally.

♥ Once soup is to a full rolling boil, add pasta. Boil for 7 to 8
minutes. Stir frequently.

Yield: 20 (1-cup) servings

Calories: 114
Percent Fat Calories: 5%
Carbohydrate: 16 grams
Protein: 10 grams

Total Fat: 1 gram
Cholesterol: 13 mg
Dietary Fiber: 1 gram
Sodium: 389 mg

Note: This soup freezes and reheats well.

**Menu Ideas: Crackers
or French bread.**

Budget
Friendly

Recipe

CORN BREAD DUMPLING SOUP

*If you like corn bread and dumplings then
you'll like this creative and unique dumpling soup!*

16 cups fat-free, reduced-
sodium chicken broth
(or 16 bouillon cubes
dissolved in 16 cups of
water.)

1 cup sliced fresh or frozen
carrots (about 2 large
carrots)

1 cup chopped celery -
optional

1 (5-ounce) can white
chicken in water

1 (6.5-ounce) package corn
muffin mix - dry (I use
Gold Medal)

3 egg whites

⅓ cup reduced-fat Bisquick
baking mix

1 (10.5-ounce) can 98%
fat-free Campbell's cream
of chicken soup - do not
add water or milk

*Super Easy
Soups & Salads*

♥ In a large soup pan, bring chicken broth, carrots, celery, and
chicken to a boil.

♥ While broth is coming to a boil, in a separate bowl mix corn
muffin mix, egg whites and Bisquick together until well mixed.

♥ Once broth is boiling briskly stir in cream of chicken soup.
Stir until well dissolved.

♥ Drop corn bread dough by rounded teaspoonfuls into boiling
broth.

♥ Reduce heat to a low boil. Cover. Cook for 10 minutes.

Yield: 18 (1-cup) servings

Calories: 93
Percent Fat Calories: 20%
Carbohydrate: 12 grams
Protein: 6 grams

Total Fat: 2 grams
Cholesterol: 5 mg
Dietary Fiber: 1 gram
Sodium: 703 mg

**Menu Ideas: Crackers, side salad
and Pumpkin Party Dessert (page 226).**

CHICKEN FLORENTINE SOUP

When I don't feel good, instead of chicken noodle soup, sometimes I make this. It's one of those soups that just helps me feel better inside.

2 pounds boneless, skinless chicken breast - cut into tiny pieces (the smaller the better)

16 cups fat-free, reduced-sodium chicken broth (or made from bouillon)

2 (16-ounce) bags frozen mixed oriental vegetables (broccoli, carrots, onions, red peppers, celery, water chestnuts and mushrooms)

1 (10-ounce) box frozen, chopped spinach

1 teaspoon garlic salt

1 tablespoon dried dill weed

¼ cup lemon juice (bottled is fine)

♥ Bring all ingredients to a full boil over medium high heat in a large soup pan. Let simmer at a low boil for 5 minutes.

♥ Serve hot.

Yield: 21 (1-cup) servings

Calories: 82
Percent Fat Calories: 7%
Carbohydrate: 4 grams
Protein: 14 grams

Total Fat: 1 gram
Cholesterol: 25 mg
Dietary Fiber: 1 gram
Sodium: 477 mg

Menu Ideas: Crackers or Tomato Biscuits (page 65 of "Busy People's Low-Fat Cookbook").

Super Easy
Soups & Salads

Budget Friendly Recipe

Pizza Pasta Salad

*Good side dish for cookouts
and picnics. Also good as a main dish.*

1   pound tri-colored spiral pasta
1   (14-ounce) jar Ragu pizza sauce
1   (8-ounce) package fat-free shredded mozzarella cheese (I use Kraft)

1   bunch green onions - chopped
2   ounces pepperoni - cut into tiny strips
¾   cup fat-free Red Wine Vinegar Salad Dressing (I use Seven Seas)

♥ Cook pasta in boiling water as directed on box for 10 minutes. Rinse cooked pasta in cold water until chilled. Drain pasta well.

♥ Mix all ingredients together.

♥ Serve as is or keep chilled until ready to serve.

Yield: 9 (1-cup) entrée size servings

Calories: 285
Percent Fat Calories: 13%
Carbohydrate: 44 grams
Protein: 16 grams

Total Fat: 4 grams
Cholesterol: 9 mg
Dietary Fiber: 2 grams
Sodium: 808 mg

Yield: 18 (½-cup) side dish servings

Calories: 143
Percent Fat Calories: 13%
Carbohydrate: 22 grams
Protein: 8 grams

Total Fat: 2 grams
Cholesterol: 5 mg
Dietary Fiber: 1 gram
Sodium: 404 mg

Menu Ideas: For a complete meal, serve with fresh veggies and fat-free salad dressing as a dip for the vegetables.

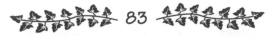

Notes

_____

_____

_____

_____

_____

_____

_____

_____

_____

_____

_____

_____

_____

_____

_____

_____

_____

_____

_____

_____

_____

Simply Delicious Side Dishes

SWEET PEAS AND PEARL ONIONS

Budget Friendly Recipe

A fast and unique way to make this recipe without a lot of fuss!

1 (15-ounce) jar pearl onions - drained

2 (15-ounce) cans sweet peas - drained

3 tablespoons reduced-fat vanilla frosting (I use Betty Crocker Sweet Rewards)

♥ Microwave onions and peas together for 2 minutes.
♥ Gently stir in frosting.
♥ Microwave another 2 minutes. Stir.
♥ Serve hot.

Yield: 7 (½-cup) servings

Calories: 109
Percent Fat Calories: 8%
Carbohydrate: 21 grams
Protein: 5 grams

Total Fat: 1 gram
Cholesterol: 0 mg
Dietary Fiber: 4 grams
Sodium: 343 mg

Menu Ideas: Any lean meat.

MAPLE YAMS

*My brother-in-law is a produce buyer.
I once asked him what the difference was between
yams and sweet potatoes. He said, "Nothing."*

1 (40-ounce) can cut sweet
   potatoes in light syrup -
   drained (discard syrup)

1 tablespoon Butter Buds
   Sprinkles - dry
¼ cup light maple syrup

♥ Break up sweet potatoes (yams) with a fork.

♥ With a hand-held mixer on low speed, mix everything together
  for 1 minute or until mashed to desired consistency.

♥ Heat in microwave for 2 minutes or until fully heated.

Yield: 6 (½-cup) servings

Calories: 150
Percent Fat Calories: 0%
Carbohydrate: 35 grams
Protein: 2 grams

Total Fat: 0 grams
Cholesterol: 0 mg
Dietary Fiber: 3 grams
Sodium: 170 mg

Menu Ideas: Lean ham, turkey breast or pork tenderloin.

Simply Delicious
Side Dishes

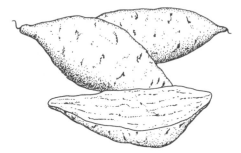

Total Time: 5 minutes.

ASPARAGUS AND MUSHROOMS

This is a tasty and quick dish!

2 (14.5-ounce) cans asparagus - do not drain
1 (4-ounce) can mushroom stems and pieces - do not drain

½ teaspoon garlic powder
2 tablespoons Promise Ultra 70% less fat margarine

♥ Mix asparagus and mushrooms together. Cover.

♥ Cook in carousel microwave for 2 to 3 minutes or until fully heated.

♥ Drain juice from vegetables. Gently toss cooked vegetables with garlic powder and Promise Ultra 70% less fat margarine. Serve hot.

Yield: 5 (½-cup) servings

Calories: 48
Percent Fat Calories: 29%
Carbohydrate: 6 grams
Protein: 4 grams

Total Fat: 2 grams
Cholesterol: 0 mg
Dietary Fiber: 2 grams
Sodium: 657 mg

Menu Ideas: Great served with any lean meat.

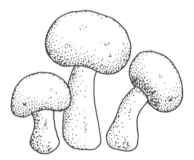

Budget Friendly Recipe

APRICOT SWEET POTATOES (YAMS)

*This flavor combination tastes wonderful
with pork tenderloin or lean ham steaks!*

1 (40-ounce) can cut sweet potatoes (yams) in light syrup - drained (discard syrup)

⅓ cup apricot preserves (with no large chunks of apricots)

♥ Spray a microwavable medium serving bowl with non-fat cooking spray.

♥ With mixer mix sweet potatoes (yams) with apricot preserves in prepared bowl until the consistency of thick mashed potatoes, but with large chunks.

♥ Cover lightly with wax paper and microwave for 2 to 3 minutes or until completely heated throughout.

Yield: 8 (½-cup) servings

Calories: 129
Percent Fat Calories: 0%
Carbohydrate: 31 grams
Protein: 2 grams

Total Fat: 0 grams
Cholesterol: 0 mg
Dietary Fiber: 2 grams
Sodium: 62 mg

Simply Delicious Side Dishes

**Menu Ideas: Great for holidays
with pork tenderloin, lean ham or turkey.**

*We have only one rule for our family
"LOVE ONLY." (If it's not loving,
you're not allowed to do it.)*

Dawn Hall

Total Time: 9 minutes.

CAULIFLOWER WITH BLUE CHEESE

Budget
Friendly

Recipe

*If you like blue cheese
salad dressing you'll like this one!*

1 (16-ounce) bag frozen
  cauliflower pieces
1 (4-ounce) can mushroom
  pieces - do not drain

⅓ cup fat-free blue cheese
  salad dressing
  (I use Wish-Bone)

♥ Mix cauliflower and mushrooms together.

♥ Microwave (in a carousel microwave) on high in a covered
  dish for 5 to 7 minutes. Drain juices from vegetables.

♥ Gently toss vegetables in blue cheese dressing.

♥ If needed, microwave 1 more minute to heat dressing.

Yield: 7 (½-cup) servings

Calories: 38
Percent Fat Calories: 0%
Carbohydrate: 8 grams
Protein: 2 grams

Total Fat: 0 grams
Cholesterol: 0 mg
Dietary Fiber: 2 grams
Sodium: 204 mg

**Menu Ideas: Great as a side entrée
with steak or chicken on the grill.**

Broccoli with Blue Cheese: Follow the Cauliflower with
Blue Cheese recipe exactly the same but substitute
1 (16-ounce) bag frozen broccoli for cauliflower.

Calories:
Percent Fat Calories: 0%
Carbohydrate: 8 grams
Protein: 2 grams

Total Fat: 0 grams
Cholesterol: 0 mg
Dietary Fiber: 2 grams
Sodium: mg

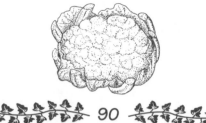

Budget Friendly Recipe

ITALIAN BROCCOLI

Talk about easy! Here ya go!

1 (16-ounce) bag frozen broccoli pieces

⅓ cup fat-free Italian salad dressing

♥ Mix ingredients well.

♥ Cook, covered, in a carousel microwave on high for 7 minutes or until fully heated.

Yield: 5 (½-cup) servings

Calories: 29
Percent Fat Calories: 0%
Carbohydrate: 5 grams
Protein: 3 grams

Total Fat: 0 grams
Cholesterol: 0 mg
Dietary Fiber: 3 grams
Sodium: 176 mg

Menu Ideas: Any Italian entrée such as lasagna, spaghetti or linguine.

Simply Delicious Side Dishes

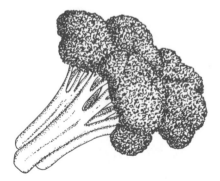

Total Time: 10 minutes or less.

HAWAIIAN PUMPKIN CASSEROLE

A unique and flavorful combination blending the tropical flavors of the Hawaiian Islands with "down home" goodness.

¼ cup shredded coconut
1 (30-ounce) can pumpkin pie mix (Libby's)

1 (20-ounce) can crushed pineapple - drain and discard 1 cup pineapple juice

♥ Preheat oven to 500 degrees.

♥ Spray a cookie sheet and a 2-quart microwavable casserole dish with non-fat cooking spray.

♥ Broil coconut on cookie sheet for 45 to 60 seconds or until toasty brown.

♥ Mix pumpkin pie mix, drained crushed pineapple and three-fourths of the toasted coconut together in prepared microwavable bowl. Microwave, covered, for 4 to 5 minutes or until fully heated in a carousel microwave.

♥ Sprinkle remaining toasted coconut on top of casserole.

♥ Serve hot.

Yield: 8 (½-cup) servings

Calories: 126
Percent Fat Calories: 6%
Carbohydrate: 30 grams
Protein: 1 gram

Total Fat: 1 gram
Cholesterol: 0 mg
Dietary Fiber: 3 grams
Sodium: 152 mg

Menu Ideas: Serve with lean ham.

Doing what is right is not always popular.

Budget
Friendly

Recipe

MASHED YAMS
WITH AN ORANGE KISS

The orange juice along with the pumpkin pie
spice gives this dish an excellent flavor!

2 (40-ounce) cans yams -
  drained (discard juice)
½ cup Egg Beaters
½ cup orange juice

½ cup fat-free Ultra
  Promise
¼ cup brown sugar
½ teaspoon pumpkin pie spice

♥ Mash yams in a large microwavable bowl.

♥ Add remaining ingredients and mix well with a mixer for about
1 minute.

♥ Microwave for 7 to 10 minutes or until set, stirring once.

Yield: 14 (½-cup) servings

Calories: 149
Percent Fat Calories: 0%
Carbohydrate: 33 grams
Protein: 3 grams

Total Fat: 0 grams
Cholesterol: 0 mg
Dietary Fiber: 2 grams
Sodium: 158 mg

Simply Delicious
Side Dishes

Menu Ideas: Great as a side dish with
lean pork, ham, chicken and of course turkey.

How much more wonderful
our world would be if we concentrated as
much energy into making friends as we do
into making money.

Dawn Hall

ZUCCHINI DE LA PARMESAN

*Zucchini (as a side dish)
never had it so good.*

1 pound zucchini - cut into ¼-inch thick slices	1 tablespoon minced garlic (I use the kind in a jar)
½ cup fat-free reduced-sodium chicken broth	½ teaspoon lemon-pepper seasoning or 1 teaspoon Spike (or salt substitute)
½ pound fresh mushrooms - sliced (for faster preparation buy the pre-cut from the produce section)	¼ cup grated fat-free Parmesan cheese (I use Kraft)

♥ Spray a 12-inch nonstick skillet with non-fat cooking spray.

♥ Over high heat cook zucchini, chicken broth, mushrooms, garlic and lemon-pepper seasoning for 5 minutes, stirring occasionally.

♥ Remove from heat. Sprinkle with Parmesan cheese.

♥ Cover. Let sit for 1 minute.

♥ Serve hot.

Yield: 5 servings

Calories: 41
Percent Fat Calories: 0%
Carbohydrate: 7 grams
Protein: 4 grams

Total Fat: 0 grams
Cholesterol: 4 mg
Dietary Fiber: 2 grams
Sodium: 125 mg

Menu Ideas: Accompanies any entrée well.

Budget Friendly Recipe

PARMESAN POTATOES

*Here's a quick and easy
way to perk up your French fries.*

3   tablespoons grated
    fat-free Parmesan cheese
½   teaspoon black pepper
1   teaspoon garlic salt

1   (1-pound) package frozen
    French fries (no more
    than 3 grams of fat per
    100 calories) - (I use
    Flavorite brand)
    Non-fat butter-flavored
    cooking spray

♥ Preheat oven to 450 degrees.

♥ Spray a cookie sheet with non-fat cooking spray.

♥ Put Parmesan cheese, pepper and garlic salt in large plastic bag. Shake until well mixed.

♥ Put fries in bag with seasonings. Shake until well coated.

♥ Pour entire contents of bag on prepared cookie sheet. Spray seasoned fries with cooking spray.

♥ Bake at 400 degrees for 20 minutes or until golden brown.

Yield: 4 servings

Calories: 111
Percent Fat Calories: 6%
Carbohydrate: 24 grams
Protein: 3 grams

Total Fat: 1 gram
Cholesterol: 0 mg
Dietary Fiber: 2 grams
Sodium: 562 mg

***Menu Ideas: Fat-free
hot dogs or lean steak or chicken breast.***

*Simply Delicious
Side Dishes*

SOUR CREAM AND CHIVES MASHED POTATOES

No one would believe that these light and fluffy potatoes aren't made from scratch!

2²/₃ cups fat-free reduced-sodium chicken broth (or made from bouillon)

²/₃ cup fat-free half & half

2²/₃ cups instant potatoes (I use Betty Crocker Potato Buds)

1 (15-ounce) can whole potatoes - drained (discard liquid)

³/₄ cup fat-free sour cream (I use Breakstone)

½ cup chopped fresh chives (or ¼ cup dried) - divided

♥ In a 2-quart saucepan, bring chicken broth and half & half to a full boil. Turn off heat.

♥ Stir in instant potatoes until moistened. Let sit for 30 seconds or until all liquid is absorbed.

♥ Meantime, mash whole potatoes in a serving bowl into tiny chunks. Microwave potato chunks for up to 2 minutes, or until potato chunks are fully heated.

♥ Stir instant mashed potatoes, warmed potato chunks, sour cream and all but 1 teaspoon chives together in serving bowl until well blended.

♥ Sprinkle reserved 1 teaspoon of chives on top.

Yield: 10 (½-cup) servings

Calories: 100
Percent Fat Calories: 0%
Carbohydrate: 20 grams
Protein: 5 grams

Total Fat: 0 grams
Cholesterol: 2 mg
Dietary Fiber: 2 grams
Sodium: 255 mg

Menu Ideas: Chicken Fried Steak (page 154) or baked chicken.

(Sour Cream and Chives Mashed Potatoes continued)

Twice Baked Mashed Potatoes: Make the Sour Cream and Chives Mashed Potatoes recipe exactly the same, except stir in ¼ cup real bacon bits. (I use Hormel. It's about ⅓ of a jar.)

Yield: 10 (½-cup) servings

Calories: 110
Percent Fat Calories: 6%
Carbohydrate: 20 grams
Protein: 6 grams

Total Fat: 1 gram
Cholesterol: 4 mg
Dietary Fiber: 2 grams
Sodium: 344 mg

Life is a lot like having air conditioning. Sometimes you don't realize "how good you have it" or "how comfortable your life is", until you "get out in the heat!"

Dawn Hall

GLAZED GREEN BEANS

Budget Friendly Recipe

Don't let the teriyaki ingredient scare you. This is a delicious and unique combination.

6 slices turkey bacon (I use Louis Rich)
1 large onion - cut into ¼-inch slices
*2 (16-ounce) bags frozen cut green beans

½ cup Kikkoman's Teriyaki Baste and Glaze (found in barbecue sauce section)
¼ cup water
½ teaspoon garlic salt

♥ *Put both bags of frozen beans in microwave on high together for a total of 10 minutes to thaw and speed up cooking time while cooking bacon.

♥ In a 12-inch nonstick skillet, cook bacon over medium heat. Arrange onion slices on top of bacon. Cook for 4 to 5 minutes. (Until bottom of bacon is crispy.)

♥ Turn bacon slices over. Continue cooking onion slices on top of bacon. Onion slices will begin to separate into ringlets. That's good. Continue cooking bacon an additional 4 to 5 minutes or until crispy.

♥ Remove bacon slices. Place bacon on paper towels to absorb fat. If desired, pat bacon with paper towels to absorb more fat. Cut bacon into ½-inch pieces.

♥ Continue stirring and cooking onion ringlets in the minimal bacon fat remaining in the skillet to caramelize the onions. (Caramelize means that the onions will get slightly brown.)

♥ Once onions have caramelized, add green beans, Kikkoman's Teriyaki Baste and Glaze, water, garlic salt and bacon pieces. Stir until well mixed. Cover. Continue cooking over medium heat for 10 to 12 minutes.

♥ Serve hot.

Simply Delicious Side Dishes

(Glazed Green Beans continued)

Yield: 12 (²/₃-cup) servings

Calories: 66	Total Fat: 2 grams
Percent Fat Calories: 20%	Cholesterol: 6 mg
Carbohydrate: 11 grams	Dietary Fiber: 2 grams
Protein: 3 grams	Sodium: 440 mg

Keeps well in a crockpot on low. Reheats well in microwave.

**Menu Ideas: Great for potlucks, buffets or
as a holiday side dish with ham, turkey or beef.**

There are three kinds of people:

Those who make things happen.

Those who watch things happening.

Those who don't know what's happening.

SWEET POTATO STICKS

Budget Friendly Recipe

These are a favorite for everyone in our family!
Not crispy like French fries, but they're definitely delicious!

1 large sweet potato   Lite salt
  Non-fat cooking spray

♥ Preheat oven to 425 degrees.

♥ Spray 2 cookie sheets with non-fat cooking spray.

♥ Scrub sweet potatoes and cut into ¼-inch fries about 3 inches long.

♥ Arrange on prepared cookie sheets. Spray fries with non-fat cooking spray.

♥ Bake at 425 degrees for 10 minutes, or until bottoms are slightly brown. (Baking time will depend on thickness of fries.)

♥ Turn over. Spray again with non-fat cooking spray. Bake an additional 7 to 10 minutes or until potatoes are tender.

♥ Sprinkle lightly with lite salt.

♥ Serve hot.

Yield: 2 servings

Calories: 142   Total Fat: 0 grams
Percent Fat Calories: 0%   Cholesterol: 0 mg
Carbohydrate: 36 grams   Dietary Fiber: 4 grams
Protein: 2 grams   Sodium: 49 mg

Menu Ideas: Great with sandwiches or fat-free hot dogs.

Sweet Potato Disks: Bake exactly the same as Sweet Potato Sticks, but cut the potato into very thin slices, like you would potato chips.

Note: Nutritional information is
exactly the same as Sweet Potato Sticks.

Simply Delicious Side Dishes

Budget
Friendly

Recipe

UNFRIED VEGGIES

*My arteries and waistline know I can't
eat fried foods. I never miss the fat or the
mess with these crispy unfried veggies!*

1	cup instant potato flakes	4	egg whites
⅓	cup Kraft Free non-fat grated topping (made with Parmesan cheese)	4-5	cups bite-sized fresh vegetables (mushrooms, onions and zucchini)
¾	teaspoon garlic salt		Non-fat cooking spray

♥ Preheat oven to 400 degrees.

♥ Spray cookie sheet with non-fat cooking spray. If desired, line cookie sheet with foil for faster clean up.

♥ Mix potato flakes, grated topping and garlic salt together in a small bowl.

♥ In a separate bowl, beat egg whites with a fork for one minute.

♥ Dip vegetables, one at a time, into beaten egg whites. Then dip into dry mixture, coating well.

♥ Place on prepared cookie sheet, making sure vegetables do not touch each other. Spray vegetables lightly with non-fat cooking spray.

♥ Bake at 400 degrees for 10 minutes. Turn over and bake an additional 5 minutes or until crispy and golden brown.

♥ Season with lite salt, if desired.

♥ Serve hot.

Yield: 8 servings

Calories: 46
Percent Fat Calories: 0%
Carbohydrate: 9 grams
Protein: 3 grams

Total Fat: 0 grams
Cholesterol: 0 mg
Dietary Fiber: 1 gram
Sodium: 189 mg

Simply Delicious Side Dishes

***Menu Ideas: Serve with fat-free
Ranch salad dressing for dipping.***

Total Time: 10 minutes or less.

Harvest Casserole

Here's a very tasty recipe you have a choice with. It's sweet enough to satisfy your sweet tooth for a dessert, but can also be served as a side dish.

1 (30-ounce) can pumpkin pie mix (I use Libby's)
1 (21-ounce) can apple pie filling
½ teaspoon ground cinnamon
½ cup quick cooking oats (I use Quaker)
¼ cup packed dark brown sugar
1 egg white
¾ cup reduced-fat Bisquick baking mix

♥ Preheat oven to 450 degrees.

♥ Spray cookie sheet and 2-quart microwavable casserole dish with non-fat cooking spray.

♥ Mix pumpkin pie mix and apple pie filling together in prepared casserole dish. Microwave in carousel microwave for 4 to 5 minutes or until completely heated through.

♥ In the meantime, mix with a pastry cutter or fork the ground cinnamon, oats, brown sugar, egg white and Bisquick until crumbly. Sprinkle onto prepared cookie sheet. Bake at 450 degrees for 3 minutes. Stir. Return to oven for an additional 1 to 2 minutes or until lightly golden brown and crunchy.

♥ Once pumpkin-apple mixture is completely heated, stir in half of the baked crumbs until well mixed.

♥ Sprinkle the remaining crumbs on top.

♥ Best if served immediately.

Yield: 11 (½-cup) servings

Calories: 192
Percent Fat Calories: 4%
Carbohydrate: 46 grams
Protein: 2 grams
Total Fat: 1 gram
Cholesterol: 0 mg
Dietary Fiber: 3 grams
Sodium: 236 mg

Menu Ideas: Turkey, chicken, pork tenderloin or lean ham.

On The Go
Entrées

Total Time: 5 to 7 minutes per entrée (half of acorn).

STUFFED HARVEST ACORN SQUASH

Budget Friendly Recipe

Beautiful to see and comforting to eat.
These can be prepared days in advance. Refrigerated
and cooked individually in the microwave for 5 to
7 minutes per acorn half when needed.

3 acorn squash - cut in half vertically and seeds removed

1 (6-ounce) box pork-flavored stuffing (I use Stove Top)

2 cups hot water

2 tablespoons Butter Buds Sprinkles -dry

¼ cup lite maple syrup

1 pound fat-free ham - cut into ¼-inch pieces

1 large apple - unpeeled and cut into ¼-inch pieces (I use a Jonathan apple, but any apple except Red Delicious is fine to use)

♥ Put acorn squash on a microwavable plate. Set aside.

♥ In a large bowl, mix stuffing (with its seasoning packet), water and Butter Buds until well mixed.

♥ Stir in lite maple syrup, ham and apple until well mixed.

♥ Fill each acorn half with prepared stuffing.

♥ Spray tops of acorn and stuffing with non-fat cooking spray. (To prevent wax paper from sticking and to help prevent drying.)

♥ Cover each stuffed acorn with wax paper.

♥ Cook on high in carousel microwave for 5 to 7 minutes per each stuffed acorn half. (To cook entire recipe: 6 halves multiplied by 5 minutes cooking time each equals cooking time of 30 minutes.)

♥ Acorn will be soft (yet slightly firm) to the touch when ready to eat. If more cooking time is needed simply cook 1 minute more per acorn half.

Yield: 6 stuffed acorn halves (1 per serving for entrée) or 12 stuffed acorn quarters (1 per serving for side dish)

Per entrée serving:

Calories: 298

Percent Fat Calories: 4%

Carbohydrate: 56 grams

Protein: 17 grams

Total Fat: 1 gram

Cholesterol: 24 mg

Dietary Fiber: 5 grams

Sodium: 1504 mg

Note: If serving as a side dish, cut each acorn half in half (¼ acorn per side dish) AFTER it is fully cooked.

Menu Ideas: As an entrée: serve with French bread, apple butter and cooked cabbage. As a side dish serve with ham, turkey or chicken entrées.

Oven method: If you'd prefer to cook in the oven, it will take a lot longer. Follow recipe exactly. Cover top of acorn half with foil. Place acorns in a glass casserole dish that has a ½ cup of water in the bottom of it. Bake at 350 degrees for 1 hour.

Crockpot method: Wrap each acorn half in foil. Place in crockpot. Put one cup of water in crockpot. Cover. Cook on high for 4 hours or on low for 8 to 9 hours.

On The Go
Entrées

We are so blessed and thank God everyday for those important to their families who have to fight for life.

Jenni Yoder

Total Time: 10 minutes or less.

TERIYAKI RICE

Fast, easy and delicious!

1 cup Kikkoman Teriyaki Baste and Glaze (found in barbecue sauce section)

½ cup chopped fresh chives (or ¼ cup dried)

¼ cup chopped fresh red or yellow bell pepper - optional

2 cups water

3 cups instant white rice (I use Minute Brand)

♥ Bring teriyaki baste and glaze, chives, bell pepper (if desired) and water to a full boil.

♥ Stir in rice. Cover. Remove from heat.

♥ Let sit 5 minutes or until water is absorbed. Fluff with fork.

Yield: 6 (¾-cup) servings

Calories: 240
Percent Fat Calories: 0%
Carbohydrate: 52 grams
Protein: 6 grams

Total Fat: 0 grams
Cholesterol: 0 mg
Dietary Fiber: 0 grams
Sodium: 1085 mg

Menu Ideas: Oriental entrées or grilled lean meats.

On The Go
Entrées

If you water it and it dies, it's a plant. If you pull it out and it continues to grow, it's a weed.

Budget
Friendly

Recipe

KIELBASA AND RICE

Sauerkraut lovers will love this dish.

1 (14-ounce) package
  fat-free Polish kielbasa
  (Butterball) - cut into
  tiny pieces

1 (16-ounce) can sauerkraut
  (rinse and squeeze dry
  with hands)

1 (14.5-ounce) can
  no-salt-added stewed
  tomatoes - cut into
  bite-size pieces

2½ cups low-sodium V8
  vegetable juice

2 cups instant rice

♥ In a large, 3-quart nonstick pan, bring kielbasa, sauerkraut, stewed tomatoes and V8 juice to a full boil, stirring occasionally.

♥ Stir in rice and cover.

♥ Remove from heat and let sit 5 minutes.

Yield: 4 (1³/₄-cup) servings

Calories: 354
Percent Fat Calories: 0%
Carbohydrate: 66 grams
Protein: 21 grams

Total Fat: 0 grams
Cholesterol: 43 mg
Dietary Fiber: 3 grams
Sodium: 1779 mg

**The easiest, quickest way to cut tomatoes
is to leave in can. Insert a knife in can and cut.**

Menu Ideas: A meal in itself. Fruit cup for dessert.

On The Go
Entrées

*Life is fullest when you
trust your own path, not try to
follow someone else's.*

CHIPPED BEEF ROLL-UPS

Budget Friendly Recipe

*Good as an appetizer or
as a wrapped sandwich for lunch.*

1 (2.5-ounce) package dried chipped beef - cut into tiny squares

1 (8-ounce) package fat-free cream cheese - softened to room temperature (I use Healthy Choice)

1 tablespoon plus 1 teaspoon Hidden Valley Ranch salad dressing mix - dry (from a packet)

¼ cup chopped fresh chives

6 (10-inch) fat-free flour tortillas (I use Buena Vida)

♥ Mixed chipped beef, cream cheese, dry salad dressing mix and chives together until well blended.

♥ Divide the mixture and spread evenly over the 6 flour tortillas. Roll each tortilla up.

♥ For a sandwich wrap, eat as is.

♥ For an appetizer, cut each tortilla into 4 sections.

Yield: 24 appetizers (1 appetizer per serving)

Calories: 46
Percent Fat Calories: 4%
Carbohydrate: 8 grams
Protein: 3 grams

Total Fat: trace
Cholesterol: 3 mg
Dietary Fiber: 0 grams
Sodium: 254 mg

Yield: 6 (1-wrap) servings

Calories: 186
Percent Fat Calories: 4%
Carbohydrate: 32 grams
Protein: 11 grams

Total Fat: 1 gram
Cholesterol: 12 mg
Dietary Fiber: 1 gram
Sodium: 1018 mg

**Menu Ideas: *Good for packed lunches as
a sandwich wrap. As an appetizer, good anytime.***

Budget
Friendly

CHILI CHEESEBURGER CASSEROLE

Recipe

*If you like Hamburger Helper
you'll really enjoy this!*

1 (7¼-ounce) box macaroni
and cheese - do not make
as directed on box
1 pound ground beef eye of
round (or Ground Meatless
or ground turkey breast)

1 (15-ounce) can 99%
fat-free Hormel chili
1 cup hot water
½ cup chopped frozen or
fresh onion

♥ Spray a large, nonstick skillet with non-fat cooking spray.
♥ Bring all ingredients to a full boil, stirring frequently. (Do NOT
precook meat.)
♥ Reduce heat to a low boil. Cover. Cook for 8 minutes, stirring
occasionally.
♥ Serve hot.

Yield: 5 (1¼-cup) servings

With ground beef eye of round:

Calories: 335
Percent Fat Calories: 16%
Carbohydrate: 39 grams
Protein: 31 grams

Total Fat: 6 grams
Cholesterol: 58 mg
Dietary Fiber: 3 grams
Sodium: 503 mg

With Ground Meatless:

Calories: 314
Percent Fat Calories: 8%
Carbohydrate: 45 grams
Protein: 28 grams

Total Fat: 3 grams
Cholesterol: 9 mg
Dietary Fiber: 6 grams
Sodium: 885 mg

With ground turkey breast:

Calories: 315
Percent Fat Calories: 8%
Carbohydrate: 39 grams
Protein: 33 grams

Total Fat: 3 grams
Cholesterol: 71 mg
Dietary Fiber: 3 grams
Sodium: 495 mg

*Menu Ideas: Green Beans and Apple Cottage Salad
(page 117 of "Busy People's Low-Fat Cookbook").*

On The Go
Entrées

Total Time: 20 minutes or less.

Open-Faced Warm Chicken Salad Sandwiches

Budget Friendly Recipe

This recipe was sent in by Angie Avers of Maumee, Ohio, with a few changes of my own. I give her full credit for this delicious and easy recipe.

1 (8-ounce) can water chestnuts - drained and finely chopped
1 (10-ounce) can chunk chicken breast in water
½ cup finely chopped fresh or frozen broccoli
⅓ cup shredded fat-free mozzarella cheese (I use Kraft)

3 tablespoons Miracle Whip Free
1 tablespoon honey mustard (I use Grey Poupon)
2 (7.5-ounce) cans refrigerated Pillsbury biscuits

♥ Preheat oven to 350 degrees.

♥ Spray a cookie sheet with non-fat cooking spray.

♥ Stir all ingredients except biscuits in a mixing bowl until well mixed.

♥ Flatten thirteen biscuits to the size of your palm. (If desired, save the remaining seven biscuits for future use.)

♥ Lay flattened biscuits on prepared cookie sheet.

♥ Top each with chicken mixture.

♥ Bake for 15 minutes.

Yield: 6½ servings (2 sandwiches per serving)

Calories: 191
Percent Fat Calories: 14%
Carbohydrate: 27 grams
Protein: 13 grams

Total Fat: 3 grams
Cholesterol: 19 mg
Dietary Fiber: 3 grams
Sodium: 633 mg

Menu Ideas: Fruit plate on the side.

SEASIDE RICE

*Our friends and family like this entrée as is,
however if you like spicier entrées you may want to serve
with a shaker of "Cajun seasoning" to sprinkle on.*

1 (14-ounce) package fat-free smoked sausage – cut into ¼-inch slices (I use Butterball)

2 (14.5-ounce) cans no-salt-added stewed tomatoes – cut tomatoes up

2 tablespoons minced garlic (I use the kind in a jar)

1 pound (41/50 count) shrimp (deveined and tails off)

1 pound imitation scallops (Louis Kemps)

2 cups fat-free, reduced-sodium chicken broth (or made from chicken bouillon)

3 cups instant rice

♥ Spray a large, nonstick soup pan or Dutch oven with non-fat cooking spray.

♥ In soup pan over high heat, bring sausage, stewed tomatoes, garlic, shrimp, scallops and chicken broth to a full boil, stirring occasionally.

♥ Remove from heat. Stir in rice.

♥ Cover. Let sit 5 minutes or until all moisture is absorbed.

Yield: 10 (1⅓-cup) servings

Calories: 245
Percent Fat Calories: 2%
Carbohydrate: 37 grams
Protein: 22 grams

Total Fat: trace
Cholesterol: 81 mg
Dietary Fiber: 1 gram
Sodium: 991 mg

**Menu Ideas: Sassy Slaw,
(page 109 in "Busy People's Low-Fat Cookbook")
and cornbread muffins.**

*On The Go
Entrées*

BREAKFAST ON A STICK

Budget
Friendly

Recipe

These can be baked ahead of time and frozen. Then just pop one into the microwave and heat for 30 to 60 seconds for a healthy breakfast on the run.

7   popsicle sticks
1   (14-ounce) package
    fat-free smoked sausage
    (Butterball)
1   cup reduced-fat Bisquick
    baking mix

1   tablespoon sugar
⅓   cup skim milk
2   egg whites
½   teaspoon vanilla

♥ Preheat oven to 450 degrees.

♥ Spray a cookie sheet with non-fat cooking spray.

♥ Cut sausage into 7 (2-ounce) pieces.

♥ Insert one popsicle stick into each sausage. Set aside.

♥ Mix together Bisquick, sugar, milk, egg whites and vanilla until dough is well blended.

♥ With hands (sprayed with non-fat cooking spray) completely coat each sausage with dough.

♥ Bake on prepared cookie sheets for 8 to 10 minutes or until golden brown.

Yield: 7 servings

Calories: 140
Percent Fat Calories: 7%
Carbohydrate: 20 grams
Protein: 11 grams

Total Fat: 1 gram
Cholesterol: 25 mg
Dietary Fiber: 0 grams
Sodium: 886 mg

Menu Ideas: Orange juice or a fruit cup.

On The Go
Entrées

Budget Friendly Recipe

TERIYAKI BEEF AND BROCCOLI

An oriental favorite among my assistants.

1 pound beef eye of round steaks - all visible fat removed
1 tablespoon minced garlic
1 (1-pound) bag frozen broccoli pieces

2 medium fresh onions - cut into quarters and separated
1 (4-ounce) can mushroom stems and pieces, drained
½ cup Kikkoman Teriyaki Baste and Glaze (found in barbecue sauce section)

♥ Cut meat across grain into very thin slices.
♥ Over high heat, cook meat, garlic, broccoli, onions and mushrooms.
♥ Cover and cook 10 minutes, stirring occasionally.
♥ Remove from heat. Drain juices from pan.
♥ Stir in Kikkoman Teriyaki Baste and Glaze.
♥ Serve hot.

Yield: 5 (1-cup) servings

Calories: 209
Percent Fat Calories: 18%
Carbohydrate: 19 grams
Protein: 24 grams

Total Fat: 4 grams
Cholesterol: 49 mg
Dietary Fiber: 4 grams
Sodium: 792 mg

On The Go Entrées

Menu Ideas: Rice and a fruit cup.

Total Time: 15 minutes or less.

SPICED HAM STEAKS

The combination of the slight sweetness and saltiness creates a terrific glaze.

4 (4-ounce) fat-free ham
   steaks (¼-inch thickness)
3 medium apples - unpeeled,
   cored and thinly sliced
1 tablespoon Butter Buds
   Sprinkles - dry

¼ cup packed dark brown
   sugar
1½ teaspoons ground
   cinnamon

♥ In a large, nonstick skillet arrange ham steaks.

♥ Arrange apple slices on top of ham steaks.

♥ Sprinkle apples with Butter Buds, brown sugar and ground cinnamon.

♥ Cover. Cook on medium heat for 4 to 5 minutes.

♥ Turn meat over. Stir apples and seasonings together until well mixed. Place apples back on top of ham steaks.

♥ Cover. Cook on low another 3 to 4 minutes or until apples are cooked and slightly tender.

Yield: 4 servings

Calories: 203
Percent Fat Calories: 0%
Carbohydrate: 34 grams
Protein: 17 grams

Total Fat: 0 grams
Cholesterol: 36 mg
Dietary Fiber: 3 grams
Sodium: 1350 mg

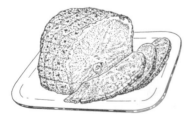

Menu Ideas: Sassy Slaw (page 109 of "Busy People's Low-Fat Cookbook") and Sweet Potato Sticks (page 100 of this book).

Budget Friendly Recipe

CHICKEN CAESAR ROLL-UP

This recipe was sent in by Mrs. Glen Miller of West Unity, OH. If you like Wendy's Caesar Pitas, you'll like these.

1   pound boneless, skinless chicken breast
1   (10-count) package fat-free flour tortillas (I use Buena Vida)
1   (10-ounce) package Dole Special Blends Italian romaine lettuce and radicchio (found in produce section)

¼ cup finely shredded Italian Parmesan cheese (I use Kraft)
¾ cup fat-free Caesar Italian dressing (I use Kraft)

♥ Cut chicken breasts into small bite-size pieces. Cook in a large, nonstick skillet, sprayed with non-fat cooking spray, until no longer pink.

♥ In the meantime, microwave tortillas until warm. (About 1 minute).

♥ After you've cooked chicken, in a bowl toss cooked chicken, salad mix, cheese and dressing together.

♥ Put ½ cup of salad/chicken mixture in center of each warm tortilla. Roll-up and enjoy!

Yield: 10 servings

Calories: 293
Percent Fat Calories: 7%
Carbohydrate: 26 grams
Protein: 15 grams

Total Fat: 1 gram
Cholesterol: 28 mg
Dietary Fiber: 1 gram
Sodium: 657 mg

On The Go Entrées

Menu Ideas: Fresh vegetable tray with fat-free Buttermilk-Dill Salad Dressing (page 52) as a dip and fresh melon.

SLOPPY RICE CASSEROLE

Budget
Friendly

Recipe

It tastes better than it sounds! Very tasty twist combining Sloppy Joes and a one dish casserole.

2 tablespoons sugar
1 (14.5-ounce) jar Not So Sloppy Sloppy Joe mix
1½ cups water
1 (12-ounce) package Ground Meatless (or ¾ pound ground beef eye of round, cooked or ¾ pound ground turkey breast, cooked)

1 (4-ounce) can mushroom pieces and stems - do not drain
3 cups instant rice

♥ Bring sugar, Sloppy Joe mix, water, Ground Meatless and mushrooms to a full boil over high heat in a nonstick 3-quart saucepan.

♥ Stir in rice.

♥ Cover.

♥ Remove from heat.

♥ Let sit 7 minutes.

Yield: 6 servings

With Ground Meatless:

Calories: 292
Percent Fat Calories: 2%
Carbohydrate: 54 grams
Protein: 16 grams

Total Fat: 1 gram
Cholesterol: 0 mg
Dietary Fiber: 3 grams
Sodium: 721 mg

With ground beef eye of round:

Calories: 305
Percent Fat Calories: 8%
Carbohydrate: 51 grams
Protein: 18 grams

Total Fat: 2 grams
Cholesterol: 31 mg
Dietary Fiber: 1 gram
Sodium: 482 mg

(Sloppy Rice Casserole continued)

With ground turkey breast:

Calories: 293
Percent Fat Calories: 2%
Carbohydrate: 51 grams
Protein: 19 grams

Total Fat: 1 gram
Cholesterol: 39 mg
Dietary Fiber: 1 gram
Sodium: 477 mg

**Menu Ideas: Sassy slaw (page 109) and
Creamed Green Beans with Ham (page 127, both
recipes are from "Busy People's Low-Fat Cookbook").**

*What you spend money on is
what you think is important. Looking at
someone's check book register can tell
where their priorities are.*

Pastor Clay

Total Time: 15 minutes or less.

REUBEN SANDWICHES

Budget Friendly Recipe

You won't miss the calories or fat in these delicious Reuben sandwiches! (Don't tell them it's low-fat and they'll never know!). Note: These sandwiches come together quickly, so have all ingredients ready!

14 slices rye bread
14 teaspoons Promise Ultra
   70% less fat margarine
2 (2.5-ounce) packages
   thin sliced lean corned
   beef (chopped, pressed
   and cooked - found next
   to chipped beef in
   refrigerated section.)

1 (14-ounce) can sauerkraut
   - rinse and squeeze dry
   with hands
7 slices fat-free Swiss
   cheese (I use Kraft)
14 teaspoons fat-free
   Thousand Island salad
   dressing (I use Wish-Bone)

♥ Preheat griddle to 400 degrees.

♥ Spread one side of each slice of rye bread with one teaspoon Promise margarine.

♥ **For each sandwich:**
   Lay buttered side of a slice of bread on hot griddle.
   Top with 4 slices of corned beef.
   Place one-seventh of sauerkraut on corned beef.
   Place one slice of Swiss cheese on sauerkraut.
   Place another slice of bread (buttered side facing up) on top of cheese.

♥ Once sandwiches are golden brown, turn over to brown other side of sandwich.

♥ Lift top slice of bread of each sandwich and put 2 teaspoons of Thousand Island dressing on meat.

♥ Replace top slice and continue cooking until golden brown.

♥ Cut sandwiches in half diagonally.

♥ Serve immediately.

On The Go Entrées

(Reuben Sandwiches continued)

Yield: 7 (1-sandwich) servings

Calories: 253
Percent Fat Calories: 21%
Carbohydrate: 38 grams
Protein: 12 grams

Total Fat: 6 grams
Cholesterol: 14 mg
Dietary Fiber: 5 grams
Sodium: 1271 mg

Menu Ideas: Fresh vegetable sticks.

QUICK FIX CHICKEN

Budget Friendly Recipe

Moist and juicy with an excellent flavor!

1   pound boneless, skinless chicken breast, cut into long ½-inch wide strips

1   cup T. Marzetti's fat-free Cole Slaw Dressing
Garlic salt - optional

♥ In a 1-gallon zip-lock bag, marinate chicken in cole slaw dressing for at least 20 minutes. (Will store up to 3 days.)

♥ Remove chicken strips and discard cole slaw dressing.

♥ Cook chicken on high heat (400 degree griddle) until brown on each side.

♥ Serve hot. Sprinkle lightly with garlic salt if desired.

Yield: 4 (3-ounce cooked) servings

Calories: 147
Percent Fat Calories: 9%
Carbohydrate: 6 grams
Protein: 26 grams

Total Fat: 1 gram
Cholesterol: 73 mg
Dietary Fiber: 0 grams
Sodium: 269 mg

Menu Ideas: Twice baked potatoes (page 145) and Sassy Slaw (page 109 both of "Busy People's Low-Fat Cookbook").

Quick Fix Steak: Make exactly the same, except substitute beef eye of round for chicken.

Yield: 4 (3-ounce cooked) servings

Calories: 172
Percent Fat Calories: 27%
Carbohydrate: 6 grams
Protein: 25 grams

Total Fat: 5 grams
Cholesterol: 69 mg
Dietary Fiber: 0 grams
Sodium: 255 mg

On The Go Entrées

(Quick Fix Chicken continued)

Quick Fix Pork Tenderloin: Make exactly the same, except substitute pork tenderloin for the chicken.

Yield: 4 (3-ounce cooked) servings

Calories: 162
Percent Fat Calories: 24%
Carbohydrate: 6 grams
Protein: 24 grams

Total Fat: 4 grams
Cholesterol: 75 mg
Dietary Fiber: 0 grams
Sodium: 243 mg

Quick Fix Turkey: Make exactly the same, except substitute turkey breast for chicken.

Yield: 4 (3-ounce cooked) servings

Calories: 148
Percent Fat Calories: 7%
Carbohydrate: 6 grams
Protein: 27 grams

Total Fat: 1 gram
Cholesterol: 85 mg
Dietary Fiber: 0 grams
Sodium: 245 mg

On The Go Entrées

Just as a body builder
loses muscle if he doesn't put
time into working out so do your spiritual
muscles weaken when you don't take time
to communicate with God.

Pastor Clay

BEEF TIPS AND ANGEL HAIR PASTA

Budget Friendly Recipe

If you like Beef Stroganoff you'll like this!

1 pound beef eye of round - cut into bite-size cubes

1 (1.2-ounce) envelope dry onion soup mix (2 envelopes per box)

3 cups water

1 tablespoon minced garlic (I use the kind in a jar - found in the produce section)

8 ounces fresh mushrooms - sliced

8 ounces dry angel hair pasta

1 (8-ounce) container fat-free sour cream

2 tablespoons chopped fresh chives - optional

♥ In a large, nonstick 3-quart saucepan, bring beef, dry onion soup mix, water, garlic and mushrooms to a full boil.

♥ Break pasta into 2-inch pieces. Stir into boiling mixture. Cook uncovered for 4 minutes, stirring frequently.

♥ Remove from heat. Stir in sour cream.

♥ Let sit 2 minutes before serving. Sprinkle with fresh chives.

Yield: 6 (1-cup) servings

Calories: 310
Percent Fat Calories: 13%
Carbohydrate: 41 grams
Protein: 25 grams

Total Fat: 4 grams
Cholesterol: 44 mg
Dietary Fiber: 2 grams
Sodium: 582 mg

Chicken and Angel Hair Pasta: Make exactly the same, except substitute 1 pound boneless, skinless chicken breast cut into bite-size pieces for the beef.

Yield: 6 (1-cup) servings

Calories: 293
Percent Fat Calories: 6%
Carbohydrate: 41 grams
Protein: 26 grams

Total Fat: 2 grams
Cholesterol: 47 mg
Dietary Fiber: 2 grams
Sodium: 591 mg

(Beef Tips and Angel Hair Pasta continued)

Pork and Angel Hair Pasta: Make exactly the same, except substitute 1 pound pork tenderloin cut into bite-size pieces for the beef.

Yield: 6 (1-cup) servings

Calories: 303
Percent Fat Calories: 12%
Carbohydrate: 41 grams
Protein: 25 grams

Total Fat: 4 grams
Cholesterol: 48 mg
Dietary Fiber: 2 grams
Sodium: 574 mg

On The Go Entrées

He is a wise man who does not grieve for the things which he has not, but rejoices for those which he has.

Epictetus

Total Time: 15 minutes.

Stir Fried Ham and Cabbage

Budget Friendly Recipe

*This is a very easy recipe not to
mention delicious, especially for cabbage lovers.*

¼ cup Butter Bud Sprinkles
  - dry
2 (16-ounce) packages pre-
  cut cole slaw mix - with big
  pieces of red cabbage
  removed

12 ounces extra lean ham -
  cut into tiny pieces
¼ cup hot water
Dash of ground black pepper
  - optional

♥ In a large, nonstick, covered skillet cook all ingredients over high heat for 8 to 10 minutes, stirring occasionally.

♥ If you desire this dish more tender, cover and continue cooking an additional 5 minutes. Serve hot.

Yield: 6 (¾-cup) servings

Calories: 116
Percent Fat Calories: 21%
Carbohydrate: 12 grams
Protein: 13 grams

Total Fat: 3 grams
Cholesterol: 22 mg
Dietary Fiber: 3 grams
Sodium: 979 mg

Menu Ideas: Serve with corn muffins.

*On The Go
Entrées*

*The best and most beautiful things in
the world cannot be seen or even touched.
They must be felt with the heart.*

Helen Keller

GARLIC BEEF

*The wonderful aroma calls everyone
to the table before it's even time to eat.*

1 teaspoon sesame oil
1 pound beef eye of round - cut into thin strips
1 (10-ounce) package frozen chopped broccoli

1 tablespoon minced garlic (I use the kind in a jar)
2 tablespoons lite soy sauce
¼ teaspoon ground pepper

♥ In a large, 12-inch nonstick skillet, cook all ingredients over high heat until beef is fully cooked.

♥ Serve hot.

Yield: 4 servings

Calories: 189
Percent Fat Calories: 30%
Carbohydrate: 5 grams
Protein: 28 grams

Total Fat: 6 grams
Cholesterol: 61 mg
Dietary Fiber: 2 grams
Sodium: 330 mg

**Menu Ideas: *Good served over rice
with Spinach Orange Salad (page 60).***

On The Go
Entrées

BEEF AND RICE CASSEROLE

Budget Friendly Recipe

*This is so good, your family will be sitting
with fork in hand asking for more, more, more!*

1 pound ground beef eye of round	1 tablespoon minced garlic (I use the kind in a jar)
1 (1.2-ounce) envelope onion soup mix - dry (2 envelopes come per box. Use only one envelope)	1 (8-ounce) package fresh mushrooms - sliced
	2 cups instant rice
2½ cups water	1 (8-ounce) container fat-free sour cream

♥ In a large, nonstick 3-quart saucepan, bring beef, dry onion soup mix, water, garlic and mushrooms to a full boil.

♥ Stir in rice. Remove from heat. Cover and let sit 5 minutes.

♥ Stir in sour cream.

♥ Let sit 2 minutes more before serving.

Yield: 6 (1-cup) servings

Calories: 283	Total Fat: 4 grams
Percent Fat Calories: 12%	Cholesterol: 44 mg
Carbohydrate: 37 grams	Dietary Fiber: 1 gram
Protein: 23 grams	Sodium: 583 mg

Chicken and Rice: Make exactly the same, except substitute 1 pound boneless, skinless, chicken breast, cut into bite-size pieces, for the beef.

Yield: 6 (1-cup) servings

Calories: 266	Total Fat: 1 gram
Percent Fat Calories: 5%	Cholesterol: 47 mg
Carbohydrate: 37 grams	Dietary Fiber: 1 gram
Protein: 24 grams	Sodium: 592 mg

On The Go Entrées

(Beef and Rice Casserole continued)

Pork and Rice: Make exactly the same, except substitute one pound pork tenderloin, cut into bite-size pieces, for the beef.

Yield: 6 (1-cup) servings

Calories: 276	Total Fat: 3 grams
Percent Fat Calories: 11%	Cholesterol: 48 mg
Carbohydrate: 37 grams	Dietary Fiber: 1 gram
Protein: 22 grams	Sodium: 574 mg

*Menu Ideas: Zucchini De La Parmesan (page 94),
Hens and Eggs Tossed Salad (page 63)
with Sweet and Sour Bacon Salad Dressing (page 53).*

*The goal . . . is the fulfillment
of something that never was on earth
before: namely your own potentiality.*

ITALIAN RICE

Budget
Friendly

Recipe

A nice alternative to spaghetti.

1 pound ground beef eye of round (or 1 pound Ground Meatless, or turkey breast)

1 (28-ounce) jar of your favorite fat-free pasta sauce (I use Ragu Light)

1 (8-ounce) can sliced mushrooms

3 cups water

3 cups instant rice

½ cup Kraft Free grated Parmesan cheese topping

♥ In a large, 3-quart nonstick pan, bring ground beef eye of round, pasta sauce, mushrooms and water to a full boil, stirring occasionally.

♥ Stir in rice and cover. Remove from heat. Let sit 5 minutes.

♥ Evenly sprinkle all servings with Kraft Free grated Parmesan cheese topping.

♥ Serve hot.

Yield: 6 (1²/₃-cup) entrée servings

With ground beef eye of round:

Calories: 353

Percent Fat Calories: 9%

Carbohydrate: 54 grams

Protein: 24 grams

Total Fat: 3 grams

Cholesterol: 41 mg

Dietary Fiber: 3 grams

Sodium: 746 mg

With Ground Meatless:

Calories: 336

Percent Fat Calories: 2%

Carbohydrate: 59 grams

Protein: 22 grams

Total Fat: 1 gram

Cholesterol: 0 mg

Dietary Fiber: 6 grams

Sodium: 1064 mg

(Italian Rice continued)

<u>With ground turkey:</u>

Calories: 337
Percent Fat Calories: 2%
Carbohydrate: 54 grams
Protein: 26 grams

Total Fat: 1 gram
Cholesterol: 51 mg
Dietary Fiber: 3 grams
Sodium: 739 mg

Menu Ideas: Garden salad with fat-free Italian salad dressing or Green Beans Italiano (page 132 of "Busy People's Low-Fat Cookbook").

On The Go
Entrées

*One is taught by experience
to put a premium on those few people who
can appreciate you for what you are.*

Godwin

Beef and Broccoli Casserole
with Zesty Cheese Sauce

Budget
Friendly

Recipe

*Move over Hamburger Helper. You won't want
"boxed" meals after eating these easy entrées!*

2½ cups Health Valley fat-free, no-salt-added beef broth (or made with beef bouillon)

1 pound beef eye of round - cut into bite-size pieces

1 cup fat-free peppercorn Ranch salad dressing (I use T. Marzetti's)

1 (10¾-ounce) can 98% fat-free broccoli cheese soup (I use Campbell's)

1 (16-ounce) bag frozen broccoli cuts

2¾ cups instant white rice

5 slices fat-free American cheese - cut into tiny pieces (I use Kraft)

♥ In a 3-quart nonstick pan over high heat, bring beef broth, beef, salad dressing, soup and broccoli to a full boil.

♥ Stir in rice. Turn off heat. Cover and let sit for 5 minutes.

♥ Stir in cheese. Cover and let sit 2 to 3 minutes more if rice is not tender. Serve hot.

Yield: 8 (1⅓-cup) servings

Calories: 302
Percent Fat Calories: 11%
Carbohydrate: 44 grams
Protein: 22 grams

Total Fat: 4 grams
Cholesterol: 37 mg
Dietary Fiber: 3 grams
Sodium: 800 mg

Menu Ideas: Fresh garden salad and lite fruit cocktail.

Pork and Broccoli Casserole with Zesty Cheese Sauce:
Make exactly the same but substitute tiny bite-size pieces of pork tenderloin for the beef.

Calories: 297
Percent Fat Calories: 10%
Carbohydrate: 44 grams
Protein: 22 grams

Total Fat: 3 grams
Cholesterol: 40 mg
Dietary Fiber: 3 grams
Sodium: 793 mg

Chicken and Broccoli Casserole with Zesty Cheese Sauce:
Make exactly the same except substitute chicken broth for the beef broth and substitute tiny, bite-size pieces of chicken for the beef.

Calories: 290
Percent Fat Calories: 6%
Carbohydrate: 44 grams
Protein: 23 grams

Total Fat: 2 grams
Cholesterol: 39 mg
Dietary Fiber: 3 grams
Sodium: 806 mg

On The Go
Entrées

Total Time: 20 minutes.

CHICKEN LINGUINE

*This fast and easy recipe comes from
the kitchen of Sandy Flick of Toledo, Ohio.*

1 pound boneless, skinless chicken breasts - cut into small bite-size pieces

1 (16-ounce) package linguine

1 (16-ounce) jar Ragu Cheese Creations Light Parmesan Alfredo

1 (10-ounce) package frozen peas

♥ Cook chicken in a large, nonstick skillet sprayed with non-fat cooking spray until no longer pink.

♥ Meantime, cook linguine according to directions on package. Drain.

♥ Microwave peas just enough to unthaw. (About 1 minute).

♥ Stir cooked chicken, cooked linguine, Alfredo sauce and peas together. Mix well. The heat from the hot chicken and linguine will heat the sauce.

♥ Serve immediately.

Yield: 8 (1¼-cup) servings

Calories: 440
Percent Fat Calories: 21%
Carbohydrate: 60 grams
Protein: 26 grams

Total Fat: 10 grams
Cholesterol: 58 mg
Dietary Fiber: 3 grams
Sodium: 574 mg

*Menu Ideas: Broccoli Parmesan
(page 142 of "Busy People's Low-Fat Cookbook") and
Italian Bagel Chips (page 39 of this book).*

Budget Friendly Recipe

ITALIAN MINI MEATLOAVES

These tasty little meatloaves are a cinch to make. They're one of my family's favorites!

½ teaspoon dried oregano
1 pound ground beef eye of round
2 egg whites
¾ cup Italian breadcrumbs
¼ cup chopped fresh or frozen onion

1 (14-ounce) jar of your favorite light pizza sauce (I use Ragu Light)
¼ cup finely shredded Parmesan cheese (I use Kraft)

♥ Spray a nonstick skillet with non-fat cooking spray.

♥ Combine oregano, ground beef eye of round, egg whites, breadcrumbs and chopped onion until well mixed.

♥ Shape into 6 mini meat loaves with hands and place in skillet over medium heat. Cover.

♥ Cook for 10 minutes or until done, turning meat over once.

♥ Pour pizza sauce over each mini meatloaf. Sprinkle with cheese.

♥ Continue cooking for an additional 5 minutes.

Yield: 6 servings

Calories: 205
Percent Fat Calories: 24%
Carbohydrate: 16 grams
Protein: 23 grams

Total Fat: 5 grams
Cholesterol: 44 mg
Dietary Fiber: 2 grams
Sodium: 557 mg

On The Go Entrées

***Menu Ideas: Tossed salad and Green Beans Italiano'
(page 132 of "Busy People's Low-Fat Cookbook").***

133

Total Time: 20 minutes or less.

ORIENTAL DINNERS

¾ pound meat* - cut into
   tiny bite-size pieces
1 teaspoon sesame oil
⅔ cup plus 2½ tablespoons
   Oriental Sauce (recipe on
   page 136)

2 (1-pound) packages frozen
   stir-fry vegetables or
   oriental vegetables (your
   favorite combination)
2 teaspoons cornstarch
1 tablespoon water

♥ Over high heat in a 12-inch or larger nonstick skillet, arrange meat in sesame oil and oriental sauce. Arrange 2 pounds of your favorite frozen oriental or stir fry vegetable combination over meat. Cover. Cook on high for 5 minutes.

♥ Stir until well mixed, making sure frozen vegetables are closer to the heat. Cover. Continue cooking over high heat for 5 minutes or until meat is no longer pink and is fully cooked.

♥ In the meantime, in a small bowl, mix cornstarch with water until well dissolved.

♥ Once meat is fully cooked, push the cooked mixture to one side of the skillet and drain the juices to the other side of the skillet.

♥ Turn heat to low. Add cornstarch mixture to juices in skillet. Stir until juices thickens.

♥ Stir vegetables and meat into thickened sauce until well mixed.

***Any extra lean, boneless, skinless meat
such as beef tenderloin, pork tenderloin, chicken breast
or shrimp can be used in this recipe.**

Yield: 4 servings

With beef tenderloin:

Calories: 286
Percent Fat Calories: 24%
Carbohydrate: 33 grams
Protein: 24 grams

Total Fat: 8 grams
Cholesterol: 53 mg
Dietary Fiber: 5 grams
Sodium: 1215 mg

On The Go
Entrées

With pork tenderloin:

Calories: 258
Percent Fat Calories: 16%
Carbohydrate: 33 grams
Protein: 24 grams

Total Fat: 5 grams
Cholesterol: 51 mg
Dietary Fiber: 5 grams
Sodium: 1211 mg

With chicken breast:

Calories: 247
Percent Fat Calories: 10%
Carbohydrate: 33 grams
Protein: 26 grams

Total Fat: 3 grams
Cholesterol: 49 mg
Dietary Fiber: 5 grams
Sodium: 1230 mg

With shrimp:

Calories: 215
Percent Fat Calories: 9%
Carbohydrate: 33 grams
Protein: 19 grams

Total Fat: 2 grams
Cholesterol: 121 mg
Dietary Fiber: 5 grams
Sodium: 1314 mg

Menu Ideas: Serve with instant rice, wild rice, or fried rice and fortune cookies (store bought).

On The Go
Entrées

Total Time: 5 minutes or less.

ORIENTAL SAUCE

*This delicious sauce is the
base for many recipes in this book.*

⅓ cup soy sauce (or lite soy sauce)

⅓ cup apple cider vinegar

⅓ cup molasses (I use light, mild flavor - Brer Rabbit brand)

5 teaspoons minced garlic (I use the already prepared minced garlic in a jar - found in produce section)

⅔ cup pineapple juice

♥ Stir together all ingredients until well mixed.

♥ Keep refrigerated until ready to use.

Yield: 1⅔ cups volume, to make 3 meals of 4 servings each - total 12 servings

Calories: 38
Percent Fat Calories: 0%
Carbohydrate: 9 grams
Protein: 0 grams

Total Fat: 0 grams
Cholesterol: 0 mg
Dietary Fiber: 0 grams
Sodium: 411 mg

Menu Ideas: Use for numerous recipes.

*I don't know why they named
it "Rogaine." They should have
named it "Regain".*

Tracy Hall

Budget Friendly Recipe

ORIENTAL PIEROGIS

This savory entrée is a delightful combination of Oriental and Polish recipes blended together for a uniquely different but flavorful dish.

1 (16.9-ounce) box Mrs. T's potato and cheese pierogis (precooked, found in frozen foods)
2 teaspoons pure sesame oil
¼ cup Kikkoman Teriyaki Baste and Glaze (found in barbecue sauce section)

1½ tablespoons lite soy sauce
1 (16-ounce) bag frozen Freshlike snow pea stir-fry with oriental noodles (it also includes broccoli, carrots and red peppers.)

♥ In a large, 12-inch nonstick skillet, cook pierogis over high heat in sesame oil until bottoms are toasty brown, about 2 to 4 minutes.

♥ Add teriyaki baste and glaze, lite soy sauce and Freshlike veggies (with oriental noodles). Reduce heat to low.

♥ Stir until well mixed.

♥ Cover and cook, stirring occasionally, for 3 to 4 minutes or until desired texture.

Yield: 4 servings

Calories: 364
Percent Fat Calories: 14%
Carbohydrate: 66 grams
Protein: 12 grams

Total Fat: 5 grams
Cholesterol: 30 mg
Dietary Fiber: 3 grams
Sodium: 1044 mg

Menu Ideas: *Good as a meal by itself, or if desired you can add a cup of any cooked, lean meat.*

On The Go Entrées

Total Time: 30 minutes.

ORIENTAL VEGETABLES AND RICE

*Don't confuse this with fried rice. This
has its own unique flavor! Also don't worry,
the little bit of sesame oil I use will give this delicious
dish **just** a **little bit** of fat, but a **lot** of good flavor!*

2 cups fat-free, reduced-
  sodium chicken broth
1 pound of your favorite
  frozen stir fry vegetables
  (I use Flav-R-Pac brand
  with carrots, broccoli,
  sugar snap peas, red
  peppers, water
  chestnuts, mushrooms
  and bamboo shoots)

1 teaspoon pure sesame oil
  (usually found in grocery
  aisle by the Mexican and
  Chinese foods)
4 ounces extra lean, thinly
  sliced ham - cut into ½-inch
  squares (lean deli ham is
  good)
2 cups instant white long-
  grain rice (I use Minute
  brand by Kraft)

♥ In a large, 3-quart saucepan over high heat, bring chicken
  broth, vegetables and sesame oil to a full boil.
♥ Remove from heat. Stir in ham and rice.
♥ Cover. Let sit for 5 minutes.
♥ If desired, serve with lite soy sauce on the side.

Yield: 4 (1½-cup) servings

Calories: 300
Percent Fat Calories: 10%
Carbohydrate: 52 grams
Protein: 14 grams

Total Fat: 3 grams
Cholesterol: 13 mg
Dietary Fiber: 5 grams
Sodium: 688 mg

Menu Ideas: This is a complete meal in itself.

*On The Go
Entrées*

Oriental Pork, Vegetables and Rice: Make recipe exactly the same, except substitute 1 pound leftover cooked pork tenderloin for the ham. Cut pork into tiny pieces. Add at beginning of recipe.

Yield: 4 servings

Calories: 402	Total Fat: 6 grams
Percent Fat Calories: 13%	Cholesterol: 67 mg
Carbohydrate: 52 grams	Dietary Fiber: 5 grams
Protein: 32 grams	Sodium: 331 mg

Oriental Chicken, Vegetables and Rice: Make recipe exactly the same, except substitute one pound leftover cooked chicken breast for the ham. Cut chicken into tiny pieces. Add chicken pieces at beginning of recipe.

Yield: 4 servings

Calories: 356	Total Fat: 3 grams
Percent Fat Calories: 7%	Cholesterol: 49 mg
Carbohydrate: 52 grams	Dietary Fiber: 5 grams
Protein: 28 grams	Sodium: 339 mg

On The Go Entrées

Reputation is what men and women think of us; character is what God and angels know of us.

Thomas Paine

ORIENTAL RICE

A delicious vegetarian dish!

Budget
Friendly

Recipe

2 (16-ounce) bags frozen stir-fry vegetables

¾ cup Kikkoman Teriyaki Baste and Glaze (found in barbecue sauce section)

2½ cups fat-free, no-salt-added chicken broth (made from bouillon is okay)

3 cups instant rice
Lite soy sauce - optional

♥ In a 3-quart nonstick saucepan bring vegetables, teriyaki baste and glaze and chicken broth to a full boil.

♥ Stir in rice. Cover. Remove from heat.

♥ Let sit 5 minutes before serving.

♥ If desired sprinkle each serving with lite soy sauce.

Yield: 6 (2-cup) entrée servings

Calories: 283
Percent Fat Calories: 0%
Carbohydrate: 60 grams
Protein: 10 grams

Total Fat: 0 grams
Cholesterol: 0 mg
Dietary Fiber: 3 grams
Sodium: 1379 mg

Yield: 12 (1-cup) side dish servings

Calories: 142
Percent Fat Calories: 0%
Carbohydrate: 30 grams
Protein: 5 grams

Total Fat: 0 grams
Cholesterol: 0 mg
Dietary Fiber: 2 grams
Sodium: 690 mg

Menu Ideas: A complete meal in itself, but if desired for a dessert, add a fortune cookie.

On The Go
Entrées

(Oriental Rice continued)

Chicken Oriental Rice: Make the Oriental Rice recipe exactly the same except add 1½ pounds cooked, diced chicken breast along with vegetables, teriyaki baste and glaze and chicken broth.

Yield: 7 (2-cup) entrée servings

Calories: 403
Percent Fat Calories: 9%
Carbohydrate: 52 grams
Protein: 38 grams

Total Fat: 4 grams
Cholesterol: 83 mg
Dietary Fiber: 3 grams
Sodium: 1254 mg

Yield: 14 (1-cup) side dish servings

Calories: 202
Percent Fat Calories: 9%
Carbohydrate: 26 grams
Protein: 19 grams

Total Fat: 2 grams
Cholesterol: 41 mg
Dietary Fiber: 1 gram
Sodium: 627 mg

Beef Oriental Rice: Make Oriental Rice recipe exactly the same, except stir in 1½ pounds raw ground beef eye of round to the pan with the vegetables and teriyaki baste and glaze. Substitute beef broth for the chicken broth. (The ground beef will be cooked by the time the dish comes to a boil.)

Yield: 7 (2-cup) entrée servings

Calories: 370
Percent Fat Calories: 11%
Carbohydrate: 51 grams
Protein: 30 grams

Total Fat: 4 grams
Cholesterol: 53 mg
Dietary Fiber: 3 grams
Sodium: 1099 mg

Yield: 14 (1-cup) side dish servings

Calories: 185
Percent Fat Calories: 11%
Carbohydrate: 26 grams
Protein: 15 grams

Total Fat: 2 grams
Cholesterol: 26 mg
Dietary Fiber: 1 gram
Sodium: 550 mg

On The Go
Entrées

(Oriental Rice continued on next page)

Pork Oriental Rice: Make Oriental Rice recipe exactly the same except stir in 1 ½ pounds raw diced pork tenderloin to pan with vegetables and teriyaki baste and glaze. Substitute beef broth for the chicken broth. (The pork will be cooked by the time the dish comes to a boil.)

Yield: 7 (2-cup) entrée servings

Calories: 362
Percent Fat Calories: 10%
Carbohydrate: 51 grams
Protein: 30 grams

Total Fat: 4 grams
Cholesterol: 58 mg
Dietary Fiber: 3 grams
Sodium: 1089 mg

Yield: 14 (1-cup) side dish servings

Calories: 181
Percent Fat Calories: 10%
Carbohydrate: 26 grams
Protein: 15 grams

Total Fat: 2 grams
Cholesterol: 29 mg
Dietary Fiber: 1 gram
Sodium: 544 mg

Shrimp Oriental Rice: Make Oriental Rice recipe exactly the same except add 1½ pounds raw shrimp (cleaned, deveined and tails off) to pan with vegetables, teriyaki baste and glaze and chicken broth.

Yield: 7 (2-cup) entrée servings

Calories: 301
Percent Fat Calories: 3%
Carbohydrate: 52 grams
Protein: 21 grams

Total Fat: 1 gram
Cholesterol: 115 mg
Dietary Fiber: 3 grams
Sodium: 1315 mg

Yield: 14 (1-cup) side dish servings

Calories: 151
Percent Fat Calories: 3%
Carbohydrate: 26 grams
Protein: 10 grams

Total Fat: trace
Cholesterol: 58 mg
Dietary Fiber: 1 gram
Sodium: 657 mg

Budget
Friendly

Recipe

BLACK BEANS AND RICE

*A southern dish made
in a fraction of the original time.*

2 teaspoons minced garlic (I use the kind in a jar)
1 teaspoon liquid smoke (found with barbecue sauce)
4 ounces extra lean cooked ham - cut into tiny pieces (lunch meat if fine)

½ cup frozen or fresh chopped onion
1 (15-ounce) can black beans - do not drain (I use Progresso)
1 cup instant long grain white rice

♥ Bring all ingredients except rice to a full boil in a 4½-quart saucepan over medium-high heat.

♥ Stir in rice. Cover.

♥ Remove from heat. Let sit 5 minutes.

♥ Serve hot.

Yield: 4 (1-cup) entrée servings

Calories: 225
Percent Fat Calories: 14%
Carbohydrate: 34 grams
Protein: 13 grams

Total Fat: 4 grams
Cholesterol: 13 mg
Dietary Fiber: 6 grams
Sodium: 736 mg

Yield: 8 (½-cup) side dish servings

Calories: 112
Percent Fat Calories: 14%
Carbohydrate: 17 grams
Protein: 7 grams

Total Fat: 2 grams
Cholesterol: 7 mg
Dietary Fiber: 3 grams
Sodium: 368 mg

**Menu Ideas: Tastes wonderful with cornbread and
Buttered Collard Greens with Ham (page 61 in
"Down Home Cookin' Without the Down Home Fat").**

On The Go
Entrées

Zany Ziti - One Pot Ziti

Budget
Friendly

Recipe

*A creamy, zany, ziti dish! I like to take this
dish to new moms. Usually they like it so much they
want the recipe. It's so easy! It becomes a family favorite!*

2¼ cups water
2 (27.5-ounce) jars Ragu
   light pasta sauce
1 (16-ounce) package ziti
   (I use Mueller's Italian-
   style ridged ziti)

1 (16-ounce) container
   fat-free sour cream
   (I use Land O Lakes)
   Kraft Free grated
   Parmesan cheese topping
   - optional

♥ In a 4-quart, nonstick Dutch oven or nonstick soup pot, bring water and pasta sauce to a full boil over medium-high heat.

♥ Add ziti. Stir until well mixed. Return to a full boil over medium-high heat.

♥ Reduce heat to a low boil over medium-low heat and cover.

♥ Cook for 25 minutes, stirring occasionally (every 3 to 4 minutes).

♥ Remove from heat. Stir in sour cream.

♥ Serve immediately with Kraft Free Parmesan cheese on the side, if desired.

Yield: 12 (1-cup) servings

Calories: 225
Percent Fat Calories: 2%
Carbohydrate: 45 grams
Protein: 9 grams

Total Fat: 1 gram
Cholesterol: 3 mg
Dietary Fiber: 3 grams
Sodium: 438 mg

*Menu Ideas: Greek Salad (page 56), French bread,
sugar-free Jell-O with Cool Whip Free topping.*

(Oven) Fried Catfish

Oow! These babies are good!

1 (6.5-ounce) package cornbread mix - dry (I use Gold Medal Smart Size)	½ cup Egg Beaters
	½ cup skim milk
	2 pounds catfish
1 cup flour	Garlic salt - optional

- ♥ Preheat oven to 450 degrees.
- ♥ Spray a cookie sheet with non-fat cooking spray.
- ♥ Mix cornbread mix and flour together. Set aside.
- ♥ In another bowl, mix Egg Beaters and skim milk together.
- ♥ Dip catfish into flour mixture, then into egg mixture, then again in flour mixture.
- ♥ Spray top of fish with non-fat cooking spray.
- ♥ Place on prepared cookie sheets. Bake until fish flakes easily when tested with a fork. (Allow 5 to 6 minutes for each ½-inch of thickness).
- ♥ If desired, sprinkle lightly with garlic salt before serving.

Yield: 6 (4-ounce cooked) servings

Calories: 257	Total Fat: 6 grams
Percent Fat Calories: 21%	Cholesterol: 82 mg
Carbohydrate: 24 grams	Dietary Fiber: 2 grams
Protein: 25 grams	Sodium: 289 mg

**Menu Ideas: Cornbread and
Slaw Salad (page 57) or Cole Slaw.**

*On The Go
Entrées*

BEEF AND NOODLES

Budget
Friendly

Recipe

*Every bit as hearty as
you remember growing up with!*

1 (16-ounce) package egg
noodles - extra wide
(I use No-Yolk)
1½ pounds beef eye of round
steak - cut into bite-size
pieces
1 (12-ounce) can fat-free
evaporated skim milk
(I use Carnation)

1 tablespoon cornstarch
½ cup chopped fresh or
frozen onion
1 teaspoon minced garlic -
from a jar
1 teaspoon lite salt -
optional

♥ Cook noodles as directed on package.

♥ In the meantime, while noodles are cooking, cook beef until
fully cooked over medium-high heat in a 12-inch or larger
nonstick skillet.

♥ In a small bowl, mix evaporated skim milk with cornstarch
until cornstarch is completely dissolved.

♥ Stir evaporated skim milk into cooked beef, along with onion,
garlic and salt. Stir constantly.

♥ Bring to a low boil. Cook, stirring constantly, for 2 minutes
or until sauce becomes thick and creamy.

♥ Drain cooked noodles. Stir cooked noodles into beef sauce.
If desired, add black pepper to taste.

**Note: If desired add one 4-ounce can of drained
mushrooms to cooked beef along with milk, onion
and seasonings. Cover. Let sit for a minute
to heat mushrooms. Serve hot.**

(Beef and Noodles continued)

Yield: 8 (1-cup) servings

Calories: 368	Total Fat: 6 grams
Percent Fat Calories: 15%	Cholesterol: 101 mg
Carbohydrate: 47 grams	Dietary Fiber: 2 grams
Protein: 30 grams	Sodium: 105 mg

Menu Ideas: Steamed broccoli and tossed salad.

Note: Leftovers of this meal freeze well. Simply microwave frozen dinner until thoroughly heated.

Pork Stew

*Another hometown favorite that many
"heart conscious" folks thought they could not eat,
but I'm happy to say, "ENJOY!"*

1½ pounds pork tenderloin -
cut into bite-size pieces
2 tablespoons minced garlic
(I use the kind in a jar)
¾ teaspoon ground sage
1 (14.5-ounce) can no-salt-
added sliced stewed
tomatoes

2 (1-pound) bags vegetables
for stew (I use Freshlike)
2 (12-ounce) jars fat-free
pork gravy (I use Heinz)
¼ teaspoon ground black
pepper

Stove top Method

♥ In a 4½-quart nonstick saucepan over high heat, bring all ingredients to a full boil, stirring occasionally to prevent burning.

♥ Once boiling, reduce heat to medium. Continue boiling for 10 to 12 minutes or until vegetables are tender, stirring occasionally.

Crockpot Method

♥ Put all ingredients in a crockpot. Stir until well mixed.

♥ Cover and cook on low for 8 to 9 hours or on high for 4 to 5 hours.

Yield: 9 (1-cup) servings

Calories: 193
Percent Fat Calories: 13%
Carbohydrate: 22 grams
Protein: 18 grams

Total Fat: 3 grams
Cholesterol: 51 mg
Dietary Fiber: 1 gram
Sodium: 487 mg

Menu Ideas: A meal in itself. If desired, sourdough bread.

CHICKEN SKILLET COBBLER

If you like pot pie, you'll like this.

1 pound boneless, skinless chicken breast - cut into bite-size pieces

1 (1-pound) package frozen mixed vegetables (peas, corn, carrots, green beans and lima beans)

1 cup frozen chopped onion (or 1 medium onion - chopped)

2 (12-ounce) jars fat-free chicken gravy (I use Heinz)

1½ cups dry pancake mix

¾ cup fat-free, reduced-sodium chicken or beef broth

♥ Spray a 12-inch nonstick skillet with non-fat cooking spray.

♥ Over high heat, cook chicken pieces until fully cooked.

♥ Add mixed vegetables, onion and gravy, stirring until well mixed. Bring to a full boil. Let boil for a couple of minutes.

♥ In the meantime, in a separate bowl, stir pancake mix and broth together to make a thick batter.

♥ Spread batter over boiling gravy. You will not have enough batter to cover entire top of gravy. That's okay. Batter spreads as it cooks.

♥ Reduce heat to a low boil. Cover. Cook for 5 to 7 minutes or until batter is fully cooked.

Yield: 4 entrée-size servings

Calories: 439
Percent Fat Calories: 6%
Carbohydrate: 66 grams
Protein: 39 grams

Total Fat: 3 grams
Cholesterol: 80 mg
Dietary Fiber: 5 grams
Sodium: 1775 mg

Menu Ideas: A meal in itself. If desired, a side salad.

On The Go
Entrées

CHICKEN PARMESAN

Budget Friendly Recipe

It sounds hard to make, but actually it's quick, easy and impressive.

4 ounces dry spaghetti or angel hair pasta

1 pound boneless, skinless chicken breast - pound to ¼-inch thick

½ cup Italian breadcrumbs

1 (25.75-ounce) jar pasta sauce (I use Healthy Choice chunky vegetable primavera)

¼ cup shredded fat-free mozzarella cheese (I use Kraft)

♥ Preheat oven to 450 degrees.

♥ Spray a cookie sheet with non-fat cooking spray.

♥ Cook pasta as directed on package. Drain.

♥ In the meantime, rinse chicken under running water.

♥ Coat moistened chicken with breadcrumbs. Place on prepared cookie sheet. Bake for 10 minutes.

♥ While pasta and chicken are cooking, microwave pasta sauce for 3 minutes in jar. (Remove lid and paper label before microwaving.) Cover top of jar with wax paper before cooking.

♥ Arrange cooked pasta on a serving plate.

♥ Put baked chicken on top of pasta.

♥ Pour pasta sauce over cooked chicken and cooked pasta.

♥ Sprinkle with mozzarella cheese.

♥ If desired, cover for a couple minutes so that the heat from the hot pasta sauce and chicken melts the cheese.

Yield: 4 servings

Calories: 343
Percent Fat Calories: 6%
Carbohydrate: 42 grams
Protein: 36 grams

Total Fat: 2 grams
Cholesterol: 67 mg
Dietary Fiber: 4 grams
Sodium: 862 mg

(Chicken Parmesan continued)

**Menu Ideas: Tossed salad with fat-free
Italian salad dressing, Parmesan Garlic Biscuits
(page 38) and sugar-free Jell-O.**

Pork Parmesan: Make exactly the same as Chicken
Parmesan recipe, but substitute one pound pork
tenderloin steaks for the chicken breast.

Yield: 4 servings

Calories: 357
Percent Fat Calories: 13%
Carbohydrate: 42 grams
Protein: 34 grams

Total Fat: 5 grams
Cholesterol: 68 mg
Dietary Fiber: 4 grams
Sodium: 836 mg

*I believe tears are a way
of communicating with God that
we ourselves sometimes don't
even understand, but He does.*

Dawn Hall

HEARTLAND CASSEROLE

Budget
Friendly

Recipe

*A basic, heartland casserole
made quickly and easily.*

1 (8-ounce) package small
pasta shells
1 cup hot water
1 (4-ounce) can mushroom
stems and pieces - do
not drain
1 (14.5-ounce) can no-salt-
added diced tomatoes in
juice - do not drain

1 (15-ounce) can ready-to-
eat reduced-fat cream of
mushroom soup (I use
Healthy Choice)
8 ounces Ground Meatless
(I use Morning Star brand)
(or ground beef eye of
round, cooked, or ground
turkey breast, cooked)
4 slices Kraft Free sharp
cheddar singles - tear
each piece into quarters

♥ In a 2½-quart or larger microwavable casserole dish, mix all
ingredients, except cheese, together until well mixed.

♥ Cover. Cook in carousel microwave on high for 10 minutes.

♥ Stir. Cover and cook another 5 minutes on high.

♥ Stir in cheese pieces until well mixed. Cover. Continue cooking
on high for an additional 5 minutes.

♥ Stir. Cover and let sit 3 to 5 minutes.

♥ If desired, ½ cup of frozen chopped green pepper or chopped
onion can be added to recipe before cooking.

Yield: 4 entrées servings

With Ground Meatless:

Calories: 372
Percent Fat Calories: 5%
Carbohydrate: 62 grams
Protein: 26 grams

Total Fat: 2 grams
Cholesterol: 3 mg
Dietary Fiber: 6 grams
Sodium: 870 mg

On The Go
Entrées

(Heartland Casserole continued)

With turkey breast:

Calories: 373	Total Fat: 2 grams
Percent Fat Calories: 5%	Cholesterol: 41 mg
Carbohydrate: 58 grams	Dietary Fiber: 4 grams
Protein: 29 grams	Sodium: 626 mg

With beef eye of round:

Calories: 385	Total Fat: 4 grams
Percent Fat Calories: 9%	Cholesterol: 33 mg
Carbohydrate: 58 grams	Dietary Fiber: 4 grams
Protein: 28 grams	Sodium: 631 mg

Menu Ideas: Green beans and a fresh clementine orange.

Ground Meatless is a vegetarian product that tastes like cooked, crumbled hamburger. If you would prefer, you can use ground turkey breast or ground beef eye of round. However, these items will need to be fully cooked before putting into the recipe. The Ground Meatless does <u>not</u> need to be cooked before adding to the recipe.

On The Go
Entrées

The fruit of the Spirit is love, joy, peace, patience, kindness, goodness, faithfulness, gentleness and self-control.

Galations 5:22-23

Total Time: 30 minutes or less.

CHICKEN FRIED STEAK

I don't know why it's called "chicken"
fried steak. It's made of beef. I bake it
until it's crispy. It is so good!

1   pound beef eye of round
    steaks - cut into
    6 (¼-inch thick) steaks
⅓ cup all-purpose flour
1   teaspoon Lawry's
    seasoned salt

¾ cup seasoned breadcrumbs
2   egg whites - beaten
2   tablespoons skim milk
1   (12-ounce) jar fat-free
    chicken gravy (I use
    Heinz) - optional

♥ Preheat oven to 400 degrees.

♥ Spray a cookie sheet with non-fat cooking spray.

♥ Pound steaks to a ¼-inch to ⅛-inch thickness. Set aside.

♥ In a bowl, stir together flour, seasoned salt and breadcrumbs.

♥ In a separate bowl, beat together egg whites and skim milk.

♥ Coat meat in crumb mixture. Dip the coated meat into egg
   mixture, then re-dip into crumb mixture.

♥ Place breaded meat on prepared cookie sheet. Spray top of
   meat with non-fat cooking spray.

♥ Bake at 400 degrees for 10 minutes. Turn over. Spray top of
   meat with non-fat cooking spray. Bake an additional 10 minutes.
   Breading will be crispy and slightly golden brown when done.

♥ Microwave gravy for 2 minutes or until fully heated. Pour ¼ cup
   gravy over each steak before serving.

Yield: 6 servings

Calories: 174
Percent Fat Calories: 19%
Carbohydrate: 14 grams
Protein: 20 grams

Total Fat: 4 grams
Cholesterol: 46 mg
Dietary Fiber: 1 gram
Sodium: 804 mg

Menu Ideas: Glazed Green Beans (page 98)
and Sour Cream and Chives Mashed Potatoes (page 96).

Budget Friendly Recipe

SPINACH FLORENTINE ITALIANO

If you're not a big spinach fan, decrease spinach to 5 ounces.

1 cup dry elbow macaroni
1 pound extra lean ground turkey breast, cooked (or Ground Meatless)

1 (28-ounce) jar low-fat spaghetti sauce (I like Health Valley)
1 (10-ounce) package frozen chopped spinach

♥ Spray a 12-inch skillet or larger with non-fat cooking spray.

♥ Stir all ingredients until well mixed.

♥ Bring to a boil. Reduce heat to a low boil and cover. Cook for 15 to 20 minutes or until pasta is tender.

Yield: 5 (1-cup) servings

With turkey breast:

Calories: 245
Percent Fat Calories: 5%
Carbohydrate: 29 grams
Protein: 29 grams

Total Fat: 1 gram
Cholesterol: 62 mg
Dietary Fiber: 5 grams
Sodium: 579 mg

With Ground Meatless:

Calories: 244
Percent Fat Calories: 5%
Carbohydrate: 35 grams
Protein: 24 grams

Total Fat: 1 gram
Cholesterol: 0 mg
Dietary Fiber: 8 grams
Sodium: 969 mg

Menu Ideas: Garlic toast, Green Beans Italiano (page 132 in Busy People's Low-Fat Cookbook.)

On The Go Entrées

ONE POT SPAGHETTI

Budget Friendly Recipe

If you like your sauce and pasta mixed together, you'll like this "whip it up fast" dinner.

1 pound ground turkey breast (or ground beef eye of round or Ground Meatless)	2 (27.5-ounce) jars Ragu light pasta sauce (or your favorite fat-free brand - I use chunky mushroom and garlic)
2 cups water	2 tablespoons grape jelly
	1 (16-ounce) package thin spaghetti - dry (broken into 3-inch pieces)

♥ Spray a nonstick Dutch oven or soup pot with non-fat cooking spray.

♥ Over high heat, stir turkey breast, water, pasta sauce and jelly together until it comes to a full boil. You do not need to precook meat. By the time it comes to a full boil, it will be cooked.

♥ Stir dry spaghetti into sauce, making sure pasta is completely covered with sauce.

♥ Reduce to medium heat. Cover. Boil for 10 minutes, stirring frequently.

♥ Turn off heat, cover. Let sit for 7 minutes.

Yield: 8 (1-cup) servings

With turkey breast:

Calories: 368	Total Fat: 2 grams
Percent Fat Calories: 4%	Cholesterol: 49 mg
Carbohydrate: 60 grams	Dietary Fiber: 4 grams
Protein: 27 grams	Sodium: 646 mg

<u>With beef eye of round:</u>

Calories: 363
Percent Fat Calories: 8%
Carbohydrate: 60 grams
Protein: 23 grams

Total Fat: 3 grams
Cholesterol: 31 mg
Dietary Fiber: 4 grams
Sodium: 645 mg

<u>With Ground Meatless:</u>

Calories: 350
Percent Fat Calories: 4%
Carbohydrate: 64 grams
Protein: 21 grams

Total Fat: 1 gram
Cholesterol: 0 mg
Dietary Fiber: 7 grams
Sodium: 884 mg

Menu Ideas: Tossed salad and garlic toast.

Total Time: 20 minutes or less.

SEAFOOD PASTA

A seafood lovers delight!

1   pound dry pasta (spaghetti, linguine, or angel hair) - cooked as directed on package.

♥ Make Seafood Chowder (page 76) recipe exactly as is, except do not add hash browns! Instead, serve over cooked pasta.

♥ If desired, sprinkle with ground black pepper before serving. Serve fat-free grated Parmesan cheese (Kraft) on the side.

Yield: 8 servings (approximately 1 cup sauce and 1 cup cooked pasta per serving)

Calories: 433
Percent Fat Calories: 7%
Carbohydrate: 71 grams
Protein: 30 grams

Total Fat: 4 grams
Cholesterol: 74 mg
Dietary Fiber: 2 grams
Sodium: 1643 mg

Menu Ideas: Tossed salad, garlic bread or Garlic Toast (page 79 of "Busy People's Low-Fat Cookbook").

On The Go Entrées

BREAKFAST PIZZA

A great way to start the day!

1 (10-ounce) can prepared pizza crust (Pillsbury - found in the dairy section)

1 cup finely chopped fully-cooked lean ham

2 cups shredded fat-free Swiss or mozzarella cheese (Kraft)

½ cup Egg Beaters

1 (12-ounce) container fat-free sour cream

½ cup chopped fresh or frozen onion

♥ Preheat oven to 425 degrees.

♥ Spray an 11x17-inch jelly-roll pan with non-fat cooking spray.

♥ With hands, spread dough to edge of pan. Arrange ham and cheese over crust. In a medium bowl, beat Egg Beaters, sour cream and onions together with a spoon until well blended.

♥ Pour over pizza.

♥ Bake 17 to 20 minutes or until pizza crust is golden brown.

Yield: 8 entrée servings

Calories: 201
Percent Fat Calories: 9%
Carbohydrate: 25 grams
Protein: 18 grams

Total Fat: 2 grams
Cholesterol: 16 mg
Dietary Fiber: 1 gram
Sodium: 701 mg

Menu Ideas: Serve with fresh fruit salad or alone with a glass of juice.

On The Go Entrées

Budget
Friendly

Recipe

ORANGE FRENCH TOAST

A zesty twist to an old time favorite.

2 (4-ounce) containers Egg
   Beaters (or 8 egg whites
   with a couple drops of
   yellow food coloring)
2/3 cup orange juice
8 slices fat-free bread
   (Aunt Millie's)

4 teaspoons powdered
   sugar - optional
¼ cup lite maple syrup
I Can't Believe It's Not
   Butter spray

♥ Spray a nonstick skillet or griddle with non-fat cooking spray and preheat to medium-high heat.

♥ With a fork, briskly beat Egg Beaters (or egg whites with yellow food coloring) with orange juice until well mixed.

♥ Dip bread slices, one at a time, into egg mixture.

♥ Arrange dipped bread slices on prepared skillet (or griddle) making sure edges of bread do not touch. Cook until bottoms are golden brown. Turn over and continue cooking until golden brown.

♥ Serve hot with 1 teaspoon powdered sugar, if desired, 1 tablespoon light maple syrup and up to 10 sprays of I Can't Believe It's Not Butter spray per serving.

Yield: 4 (2-slice) servings

Calories: 215
Percent Fat Calories: 0%
Carbohydrate: 42 grams
Protein: 11 grams

Total Fat: 0 grams
Cholesterol: 0 mg
Dietary Fiber: 2 grams
Sodium: 468 mg

On The Go Entrées

Menu Ideas:
Fruit cup or orange slices.
Coffee or herbal tea.

MUSHROOM AND ONION FRITTATA

Budget Friendly Recipe

Terrific for breakfast, brunch, lunch
or dinner! Taste like a thin, crustless quiche.

1 cup chopped onion (for faster preparation, I use frozen chopped onion)

8 ounces fresh mushrooms - sliced (for faster preparation I buy the pre-cut from the produce section)

2 teaspoons minced garlic (I use the kind in a jar)

½ teaspoon dried basil - crushed

2 tablespoons Butter Buds Sprinkles - dry

1 cup Egg Beaters

1 tablespoon Kraft Free grated Parmesan cheese topping

♥ Preheat oven to 450 degrees.

♥ Spray nonstick 12-inch skillet with non-fat cooking spray.

♥ Over high heat cook onion, mushrooms, garlic and basil until fully cooked, about 3 to 4 minutes. Stir frequently.

♥ Once fully cooked, stir in Butter Buds.

♥ Pour Egg Beaters over cooked mixture. Cook for one minute.

♥ Put entire pan into oven. Bake, uncovered, for 4 to 5 minutes or until fully set. Sprinkle with Kraft free non-fat grated topping.

♥ Invert frittata onto a large serving plate. (A cake plate works well).

Yield: 4 servings

Calories: 75
Percent Fat Calories: 0%
Carbohydrate: 12 grams
Protein: 8 grams

Total Fat: 0 grams
Cholesterol: 0 mg
Dietary Fiber: 1 gram
Sodium: 312 mg

Menu Ideas: Fresh sliced tomatoes and English muffins.

On The Go Entrées

Budget
Friendly

Recipe

FRENCH TOAST STICKS

*My children like the high fat version of
these at fast food restaurants. So I created my own
just as yummy and fun to eat, but a whole lot healthier.*

12 slices thick-sliced Texas
toast bread (any thick-
sliced white bread)

2 (4-ounce) containers Egg
Beaters (or 8 egg whites
with a couple of drops
yellow food coloring)
2/3 cup skim milk

♥ Preheat a nonstick griddle to 400 degrees or nonstick
skillet to high heat. Spray with non-fat cooking spray.

♥ Cut each slice of bread into 3 strips. Set aside.

♥ In a mixing bowl, mix Egg Beaters and skim milk together
until well blended.

♥ Lightly dip the bread sticks (one at a time) into egg mixture.

♥ Cook on hot griddle until bottoms are toasty brown. Turn a
quarter turn until all 4 sides of the French toast stick are
cooked.

♥ Serve with lite maple syrup on the side for dipping.

This finger food is easy to clean-up after.

Yield: 12 (3-piece) servings

Calories: 134
Percent Fat Calories: 11%
Carbohydrate: 23 grams
Protein: 6 grams

Total Fat: 2 grams
Cholesterol: 1 mg
Dietary Fiber: 1 gram
Sodium: 280 mg

Menu Ideas: Orange juice or a fruit cup.

Cinnamon French Toast Sticks: Make exactly the same
as French Toast Sticks but also add 1 teaspoon ground
cinnamon to the egg mixture. Stir until well mixed.

**Note: Same nutritional
information at French Toast Sticks.**

On The Go
Entrées

Total Time: 20 minutes or less.

BREAKFAST SCRAMBLE

Don't limit this great entrée to only breakfast. . .it's hearty enough for dinner! Great for brunch, too!

2 tablespoons fat-free, reduced-sodium chicken broth	½ cup frozen chopped onion (or ½ medium onion - chopped)
1 pound frozen fat-free hash browns	1 cup Egg Beaters
8 ounces extra lean honey smoked ham (from the deli)	1 tablespoon fresh chives - chopped
	1 cup shredded fat-free cheddar cheese (Kraft)

♥ Spray a nonstick 12-inch skillet with non-fat cooking spray.

♥ Combine chicken broth, hash browns, ham and onion in skillet.

♥ Cover and cook over medium heat for 10 minutes or until potatoes are tender, stirring frequently.

♥ Add Egg Beaters and chives. Cook, stirring frequently, until eggs are fully cooked.

♥ Remove from heat and gently stir in cheese.

Yield: 4 servings

Calories: 246	Total Fat: 4 grams
Percent Fat Calories: 13%	Cholesterol: 32 mg
Carbohydrate: 24 grams	Dietary Fiber: 2 grams
Protein: 28 grams	Sodium: 1173 mg

Menu Ideas:
Orange juice or fresh fruit cup, and ½ of an English Muffin with jam.

(Breakfast Scramble continued)

Southwestern Breakfast Scramble: Follow Breakfast Scramble recipe exactly, except omit the chives and onions. Once completely cooked, heat one cup of your favorite salsa in the microwave for one minute (or until fully heated). Pour ¼ cup salsa over each serving.

Yield: 4 servings

Calories: 258
Percent Fat Calories: 13%
Carbohydrate: 25 grams
Protein: 28 grams

Total Fat: 4 grams
Cholesterol: 32 mg
Dietary Fiber: 2 grams
Sodium: 1452 mg

Italian Breakfast Scramble: Follow Breakfast Scramble recipe exactly except omit chives. Once completely cooked, heat one cup of your favorite fat-free spaghetti sauce in the microwave for one minute (or until fully heated). Pour ¼ cup spaghetti sauce over each serving. (I use Ragu Light pasta sauce.)

Yield: 4 servings

Calories: 267
Percent Fat Calories: 12%
Carbohydrate: 29 grams
Protein: 29 grams

Total Fat: 4 grams
Cholesterol: 32 mg
Dietary Fiber: 3 grams
Sodium: 1368 mg

On The Go Entrées

Friendship is love with understanding.

Ancient Proverb

CITRUS PANCAKES

A tasty twist to an old time favorite.

2   egg whites
1¼ cups orange juice
2   cups reduced-fat
    Bisquick baking mix

36 sprays I Can't Believe
    It's Not Butter
1   tablespoon plus 1 teaspoon
    powdered sugar

♥ Preheat nonstick griddle or skillet to 400 degrees and spray with non-fat cooking spray.

♥ In a medium bowl, beat egg whites and orange juice together until well blended.

♥ Stir in Bisquick mix. Batter may be lumpy.

♥ Pour ¼ cup batter onto prepared griddle (or skillet).

♥ Cook until top of pancake is covered with bubbles and edges look dry.

♥ Turn pancake over and cook other side just until lightly browned.

♥ Serve with 9 sprays of I Can't Believe It's Not Butter and 1 teaspoon powdered sugar per serving.

Yield: 4 (3-pancake) servings

Calories: 280
Percent Fat Calories: 13%
Carbohydrate: 53 grams
Protein: 7 grams

Total Fat: 4 grams
Cholesterol: 0 mg
Dietary Fiber: 1 gram
Sodium: 725 mg

Menu Ideas: Scrambled eggs (made with Egg Beaters) and skim milk.

On The Go Entrées

Speedy Sweets

Index of Speedy Sweets continued on page 166

Speedy
Sweets continued

Budget
Friendly

Recipe

BREAKFAST PARFAIT

This is one of my all time favorites!
Good anytime of the day!

1 (8-ounce) container fat-
free yogurt - any flavor
(I like strawberry)

1 small banana - cut into
thin slices
½ cup 98% fat-free granola
(I use Health Valley)

♥ Spoon half of the yogurt into the bottom of two pretty parfait glasses. (If you don't have parfait glasses, any wide mouthed glass will be fine as long as it holds 10 ounces.)

♥ Top with half the banana slices.

♥ Sprinkle half the granola on top of bananas.

♥ Repeat layers with remaining yogurt, banana slices and granola.

♥ If you like, save a little yogurt to top off each dessert.

Yield: 2 (1¼-cup) servings

Calories: 197
Percent Fat Calories: 0%
Carbohydrate: 43 grams
Protein: 7 grams

Total Fat: 0 grams
Cholesterol: 3 mg
Dietary Fiber: 3 grams
Sodium: 104 mg

Menu Ideas: A meal in itself.

Speedy
Sweets

Mocha Mousse

Budget
Friendly

Recipe

*This thick, creamy dessert
is too rich to be called pudding!*

2 teaspoons instant coffee
1 tablespoon hot water
2 (8-ounce) packages
  fat-free cream cheese -
  softened (I use Healthy
  Choice)

½ cup Hershey's lite
  chocolate syrup
1 (8-ounce) container Cool
  Whip Free - thawed
2 tablespoons powdered
  sugar

♥ Dissolve coffee in hot water.

♥ With a hand-held mixer on medium speed, in a medium bowl beat dissolved coffee, cream cheese, and chocolate syrup until smooth and creamy.

♥ Fold in Cool Whip Free and powdered sugar.

♥ Keep chilled until ready to serve.

Yield: 9 (½-cup) servings

Calories: 117
Percent Fat Calories: 0%
Carbohydrate: 19 grams
Protein: 8 grams

Total Fat: 0 grams
Cholesterol: 5 mg
Dietary Fiber: 0 grams
Sodium: 278 mg

Speedy
Sweets

Menu Ideas: Tasty dip for pretzels or spread on graham crackers. Also good alone as a thick mousse.

Budget
Friendly

Recipe

BREAKFAST TRIFLE

*Vonda and Todd, (D.J.'s for YES FM, 89.3
in Toledo, Ohio) gave this "TWO BIG THUMBS UP!"*

1 (32-ounce) container fat-free strawberry yogurt	1 pound fresh strawberries - cleaned and halved
1 (12.5-ounce) box 98% fat-free granola (I use Health Valley)	1 (32-ounce) container fat-free vanilla yogurt

♥ Spread strawberry yogurt in the bottom of a glass bowl.

♥ Sprinkle half the granola over yogurt.

♥ Arrange strawberries on top.

♥ Spread vanilla yogurt over strawberries.

♥ Sprinkle remaining granola on top.

♥ Serve chilled.

**Note: Banana, fresh blueberries and other tasty
flavors can be substituted for an array of different
Breakfast Trifle combinations.**

Yield: 11 (8-ounce) servings

Calories: 270
Percent Fat Calories: 3%
Carbohydrate: 58 grams
Protein: 11 grams

Total Fat: 1 gram
Cholesterol: 4 mg
Dietary Fiber: 4 grams
Sodium: 161 mg

Speedy
Sweets

**Note: For a lower calorie version,
substitute sugar-free, fat-free
yogurts, reducing calories to
201 and carbohydrates to
41 grams. Remaining nutrients
stay about the same.**

Menu Ideas: Breakfast buffets or brunch buffets.

MOLASSES COOKIES

If you like the taste of molasses you'll love these!

1   egg white
⅓ cup molasses
1   cup reduced-fat Bisquick baking mix

¼ cup packed dark brown sugar
1   tablespoon powdered sugar

♥ Preheat oven to 400 degrees.

♥ Spray 2 cookie sheets with non-fat cooking spray. Set aside.

♥ Mix all ingredients, except powdered sugar, in a medium bowl with a spatula until well mixed.

♥ Drop by rounded teaspoonfuls onto prepared cookie sheets.

♥ Bake at 400 degrees for 4 minutes or until bottoms are lightly golden brown.

♥ Sprinkle or sift tops of cookies with powdered sugar.

Yield: 24 cookies (Nutritional information per cookie)

Calories: 42
Percent Fat Calories: 0%
Carbohydrate: 9 grams
Protein: 1 gram

Total Fat: 0 grams
Cholesterol: 0 mg
Dietary Fiber: 0 grams
Sodium: 63 mg

Menu Ideas: Snacks or lunches.

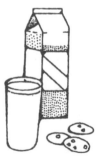

SOUR CREAM COOKIES

*A slight variation to the traditional
sugar cookie. It tastes very good!*

⅓ cup plus 1 tablespoon fat-
   free sour cream
1 cup reduced-fat Bisquick
   baking mix

½ cup powdered sugar
1 tablespoon skim milk
1 tablespoon granulated
   sugar

♥ Preheat oven to 400 degrees.

♥ Spray 2 cookie sheets with non-fat cooking spray. Set aside.

♥ Mix all ingredients, except granulated sugar, together in a
  medium bowl with a spatula until well mixed.

♥ Drop by rounded teaspoonfuls onto prepared cookie sheets.
  Sprinkle tops lightly with granulated sugar.

♥ Bake at 400 degrees for 5 minutes or until bottoms are
  lightly golden brown.

Yield: 24 cookies (Nutritional information per cookie)

Calories: 35
Percent Fat Calories: 8%
Carbohydrate: 7 grams
Protein: 1 gram

Total Fat: trace
Cholesterol: 0 mg
Dietary Fiber: 0 grams
Sodium: 62 mg

Menu Ideas: Snacks or lunches.

Speedy
Sweets

Total Time: 10 minutes or less.

ORANGE SUGAR COOKIES

*An old time favorite! These soft,
moist cookies are a sure winner with our family!*

COOKIES

⅓ cup plus 1 tablespoon
    orange juice
1 cup reduced-fat Bisquick
    baking mix

¼ cup sugar
1 teaspoon orange extract
    (found next to vanilla
    extract)

FROSTING

2 tablespoons reduced-fat
    vanilla frosting (I use
    Betty Crocker Sweet
    Rewards)

2 drops orange extract

♥ Preheat oven to 400 degrees.

♥ Spray 2 cookie sheets with non-fat cooking spray. Set aside.

♥ Mix all cookie ingredients together in a medium bowl with a
spatula until well mixed.

♥ Drop by rounded teaspoonfuls onto prepared cookie sheets.

♥ Bake at 400 degrees for 4 minutes or until bottoms are
lightly golden brown.

♥ While cookies are baking, microwave frosting for 15 seconds,
just enough to melt. Stir in orange extract. Drizzle frosting
over warm, baked cookies.

Yield: 24 cookies (Nutritional information per cookie)

Calories: 35
Percent Fat Calories: 0%
Carbohydrate: 7 grams
Protein: 0 grams

Total Fat: 0 grams
Cholesterol: 0 mg
Dietary Fiber: 0 grams
Sodium: 61 mg

Menu Ideas: A light dessert or snack.

Speedy
Sweets

Lemonade Cookies: Make exactly as orange cookies, but substitute lemonade for the orange juice and also substitute lemon extract for the orange extract.

Yield: 24 cookies (Nutritional information per cookie)

Calories: 35
Percent Fat Calories: 0%
Carbohydrate: 7 grams
Protein: 0 grams

Total Fat: 0 grams
Cholesterol: 0 mg
Dietary Fiber: 0 grams
Sodium: 61 mg

Speedy Sweets

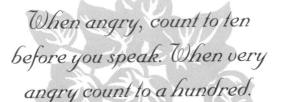

When angry, count to ten before you speak. When very angry count to a hundred.

Thomas Jefferson

Total Time: 9 minutes.

Coconut Cookies

Budget Friendly Recipe

These coconut cookies are incredibly delicious.

1 teaspoon imitation coconut extract (Durkee brand - found by the vanilla)

⅓ cup virgin piña colada mix (I use Lemix fat-free)

1 cup reduced-fat Bisquick baking mix

¼ cup sugar

1½ tablespoons shredded coconut

- ♥ Preheat oven to 400 degrees.
- ♥ Spray 2 cookie sheets with non-fat cooking spray. Set aside.
- ♥ Mix coconut flavoring, piña colada mix, Bisquick and sugar together until well blended with a spoon in a medium-sized bowl.
- ♥ Drop by rounded teaspoonfuls onto prepared cookie sheets.
- ♥ Sprinkle tops of cookies lightly with coconut.
- ♥ Bake at 400 degrees for 4 minutes or until bottoms are golden brown.

Yield: 24 cookies (Nutritional information per cookie)

Calories: 32
Percent Fat Calories: 14%
Carbohydrate: 6 grams
Protein: 0 grams

Total Fat: trace
Cholesterol: 0 mg
Dietary Fiber: 0 grams
Sodium: 58 mg

Menu Ideas: A light dessert or snack.

Speedy Sweets

Budget
Friendly

Recipe

CHOCOLATE COCONUT COOKIES

Definitely rated "A+".

1 (18.25-ounce) German
chocolate super moist
cake mix - dry - do not
make as directed on box
(I use Betty Crocker)
2 (4-ounce) containers Egg
Beaters (or 8 egg whites)

1 teaspoon imitation
coconut extract
(I use Durkee brand)
3/4 cup virgin piña colada mix
(I use Lemix brand -
fat-free)
1/4 cup shredded coconut

♥ Preheat oven to 400 degrees.

♥ Spray 4 cookie sheets with non-fat cooking spray. Set aside.

♥ Mix cake mix, Egg Beaters, coconut extract and piña colada
mix together with a spoon until well blended in a medium-
sized bowl.

♥ Drop by rounded teaspoonfuls onto prepared cookie sheets.

♥ Sprinkle tops lightly with coconut.

♥ Bake at 400 degrees for 4 to 5 minutes or until bottoms are
lightly browned.

Yield: 78 cookies (Nutritional information per cookie)

Calories: 32
Percent Fat Calories: 20%
Carbohydrate: 6 grams
Protein: 1 gram

Total Fat: 1 gram
Cholesterol: 0 mg
Dietary Fiber: 0 grams
Sodium: 46 mg

Menu Ideas: A light dessert or snack.

*I'd rather fail doing my best,
than to cheat to succeed.*

Speedy
Sweets

Total Time: 10 minutes or less.

APPLE CINNAMON COOKIES (SOFT)

Budget
Friendly

Recipe

A good flavor and good treat!

⅓ cup plus 1 tablespoon
skim milk
1 cup reduced-fat Bisquick
baking mix
¼ cup packed dark brown
sugar

1 teaspoon ground cinnamon
1 cup chopped Granny
Smith apple (Or any good
baking apple. Red
Delicious are NOT good
baking apples.)

♥ Preheat oven to 400 degrees.

♥ Spray 2 cookie sheets with non-fat cooking
spray. Set aside.

♥ Mix all ingredients together in a medium bowl with a spoon
until well mixed.

♥ Drop by rounded teaspoonfuls onto prepared cookie sheets.

♥ Bake at 400 degrees for 4 minutes or until lightly golden
brown on bottom.

Yield: 24 cookies (Nutritional information per cookie)

Calories: 32
Percent Fat Calories: 10%
Carbohydrate: 7 grams
Protein: 1 gram

Total Fat: trace
Cholesterol: 0 mg
Dietary Fiber: 0 grams
Sodium: 61 mg

Menu Ideas: A light dessert or snack.

Cinnamon Soft Cookies: Make exactly the same as Apple
Cinnamon Cookies except omit chopped apple. Sprinkle
tops lightly with cinnamon if desired.

Yield: 24 cookies (Nutritional information per cookie)

Calories: 29
Percent Fat Calories: 10%
Carbohydrate: 6 grams
Protein: 1 gram

Total Fat: trace
Cholesterol: 0 mg
Dietary Fiber: 0 grams
Sodium: 61 mg

Speedy Sweets

Budget
Friendly

Recipe

VERY VANILLA COOKIES

Very simple and very easy.
If you like sugar cookies, you'll like these.

⅓ cup plus 1 tablespoon
  skim milk
1 cup reduced-fat Bisquick
   baking mix
¼ cup sugar

1 teaspoon vanilla
2 tablespoons reduced-fat
   vanilla frosting (I use
   Betty Crocker Sweet
   Rewards)

♥ Preheat oven to 400 degrees.

♥ Spray 2 cookie sheets with non-fat cooking spray. Set aside.

♥ Mix all ingredients, except frosting, together in a medium
  bowl with a spoon until well mixed.

♥ Drop by rounded teaspoonfuls onto prepared cookie sheets.

♥ Bake at 400 degrees for 4 minutes or until lightly golden
  brown on bottom.

♥ Microwave frosting 10 to 15 seconds, just enough to melt.
  Drizzle frosting over cookies.

Yield: 24 cookies (Nutritional information per cookie)

Calories: 34
Percent Fat Calories: 12%
Carbohydrate: 7 grams
Protein: 1 gram

Total Fat: trace
Cholesterol: 0 mg
Dietary Fiber: 0 grams
Sodium: 63 mg

Menu Ideas: Good after any meal.

Almond Flavored Cookies: Make Very Vanilla Cookies
exactly the same except substitute almond extract for
the vanilla. Also, add 2 drops of almond extract to the
frosting and mix well before microwaving.

Yield: 24 cookies (Nutritional information per cookie)

Calories: 35
Percent Fat Calories: 12%
Carbohydrate: 7 grams
Protein: 1 gram

Total Fat: trace
Cholesterol: 0 mg
Dietary Fiber: 0 grams
Sodium: 63 mg

Speedy
Sweets

Total Time: 10 minutes or less for 2 dozen,
21 minutes or less for 78 cookies.

CHOCOLATE SOUR CREAM COOKIES

A chocolate lovers delight!

1 (18.25-ounce) box
reduced-fat devil's food
cake mix - dry - do not
make as directed on box
(I use Betty Crocker
Sweet Rewards)

2 (4-ounce) containers Egg
Beaters (or 8 egg whites)
½ cup non-fat sour cream

♥ Preheat oven to 400 degrees.

♥ Spray 4 cookie sheets with non-fat cooking spray. Set aside.

♥ Mix all ingredients together in a medium bowl with a spatula until well mixed.

♥ Drop by rounded teaspoonfuls onto prepared cookie sheets.

♥ Bake at 400 degrees for 4 minutes or until center is set.

Yield: 78 cookies (Nutritional information per cookie)

Calories: 30
Percent Fat Calories: 17%
Carbohydrate: 6 grams
Protein: 1 gram

Total Fat: 1 gram
Cholesterol: 0 mg
Dietary Fiber: 0 grams
Sodium: 57 mg

**Menu Ideas: A light dessert
or a yummy after school snack.**

Double Chocolate Sour Cream Cookies: Make recipe exactly the same as Chocolate Sour Cream Cookies. Microwave ¼ cup reduced-fat chocolate frosting (Betty Crocker Sweet Rewards) for 15 to 25 seconds or until melted. Lightly drizzle frosting over baked cookies.

Yield: 78 cookies (Nutritional information per cookie)

Calories: 33
Percent Fat Calories: 17%
Carbohydrate: 6 grams
Protein: 1 gram

Total Fat: 1 gram
Cholesterol: 0 mg
Dietary Fiber: 0 grams
Sodium: 60 mg

Chocolate Coconut Sour Cream Cookies: Make recipe exactly the same as Chocolate Sour Cream Cookies except stir in 1 teaspoon coconut extract to batter with other ingredients. Sprinkle with shredded coconut before baking (using ¼ cup total).

Yield: 78 cookies (Nutritional information per cookie)

Calories: 31
Percent Fat Calories: 18%
Carbohydrate: 6 grams
Protein: 1 gram

Total Fat: 1 gram
Cholesterol: 0 mg
Dietary Fiber: 0 grams
Sodium: 58 mg

Speedy Sweets

CAPPUCCINO COOKIES

Budget
Friendly

Recipe

These babies are excellent!

1 (18.25-ounce) box
reduced-fat devil's food
cake mix (Betty Crocker
Sweet Rewards) - dry -
do not make as directed
on box

1 tablespoon instant coffee
1 teaspoon ground
cinnamon
¾ cup skim milk
2 (4-ounce) containers Egg
Beaters (or 8 egg whites)

♥ Preheat oven to 400 degrees.

♥ Spray 4 cookie sheets with non-fat cooking spray. Set aside.

♥ Mix all ingredients together with a spatula until well blended in a medium-sized bowl.

♥ Drop by rounded heaping teaspoonfuls onto prepared cookie sheets.

♥ Bake at 400 degrees for 5 minutes or until centers are set.

Yield: 48 cookies (Nutritional information per cookie)

Calories: 47
Percent Fat Calories: 17%
Carbohydrate: 9 grams
Protein: 1 gram

Total Fat: 1 gram
Cholesterol: 0 mg
Dietary Fiber: 0 grams
Sodium: 93 mg

Menu Ideas: Good for light teas, snacks or lunches.

Double Chocolate Cappuccino Cookies: Make the Cappuccino Cookies recipe exactly the same and stir in 1 cup candy-coated semi-sweet chocolate bits. (Hershey's)

Yield: 48 cookies (Nutritional information per cookie)

Calories: 72
Percent Fat Calories: 27%
Carbohydrate: 12 grams
Protein: 1 gram

Total Fat: 2 grams
Cholesterol: 0 mg
Dietary Fiber: 1 gram
Sodium: 93 mg

(Cappuccino Cookies continued)

Amaretto Cappuccino Cookies: Make the Cappuccino Cookies recipe exactly the same and stir in 2 teaspoons almond extract.

Yield: 48 cookies (Nutritional information per cookie)

Calories: 48
Percent Fat Calories: 17%
Carbohydrate: 9 grams
Protein: 1 gram

Total Fat: 1 gram
Cholesterol: 0 mg
Dietary Fiber: 0 grams
Sodium: 93 mg

*Life is a gift from God.
What we make of our life is
a gift we give to God.*

Cinnamon Drops

Budget Friendly Recipe

*These little cookies are just right for curbing
a sweet tooth when you need just a little something.*

1 cup Egg Beaters	¼ teaspoon ground cloves
1¾ cups powdered sugar	1¾ cups all-purpose flour
1½ teaspoons vanilla extract	198 cinnamon imperials candies (red hots)
½ teaspoon ground cinnamon	

♥ Preheat oven to 350 degrees.

♥ Spray cookie sheets with non-fat cooking spray. Set aside.

♥ In a large bowl, use an electric mixer to beat Egg Beaters, powdered sugar and vanilla until thick.

♥ Gradually blend in cinnamon, cloves and flour and stir until well blended.

♥ Drop by rounded teaspoonfuls onto prepared cookie sheets.

♥ Place 3 cinnamon candies on each cookie.

♥ Bake for 8 to 9 minutes or until bottoms are lightly colored.

Yield: 66 cookies (Nutritional information per cookie)

Calories: 30	Total Fat: 0 grams
Percent Fat Calories: 0%	Cholesterol: 0 mg
Carbohydrate: 7 grams	Dietary Fiber: 0 grams
Protein: 1 gram	Sodium: 6 mg

Menu Ideas: Snacks or lunches.

Speedy Sweets

Brown Sugar Drops: Make Cinnamon Drops recipe exactly the same except omit candies and instead sprinkle top of each cookie with ¼ teaspoon dark brown sugar before baking. Bake 8 to 9 minutes.

Yield: 66 cookies (Nutritional information per cookie)

Calories: 31
Percent Fat Calories: 0%
Carbohydrate: 7 grams
Protein: 1 gram

Total Fat: 0 grams
Cholesterol: 0 mg
Dietary Fiber: 0 grams
Sodium: 7 mg

Cherry Drops: Make Cinnamon Drops recipe exactly the same except omit candies and instead put a maraschino cherry half in the center of each cookie before baking. Bake 8 to 9 minutes.

Yield: 66 cookies (Nutritional information per cookie)

Calories: 32
Percent Fat Calories: 0%
Carbohydrate: 7 grams
Protein: 1 gram

Total Fat: 0 grams
Cholesterol: 0 mg
Dietary Fiber: 0 grams
Sodium: 6 mg

Speedy
Sweets

*Home is a place where the great
are small, and the small are great.*

Anonymous

DELICIOUS DATE COOKIES

Budget
Friendly

Recipe

I hit a "BULLSEYE" when I created these!
*The recipe title says it all! I **love** the flavor combination!*

⅓ cup plus 1 tablespoon
Sunny Delight citrus
beverage or orange juice
1 cup reduced-fat Bisquick
baking mix
¼ cup packed dark brown
sugar

1 teaspoon ground
cinnamon
½ cup chopped dates (Dole
brand - found in baking
section)

♥ Preheat oven to 400 degrees.

♥ Spray 2 cookie sheets with non-fat cooking spray. Set aside.

♥ Mix all ingredients together in a medium bowl with a spoon until well mixed.

♥ Drop by rounded teaspoonfuls onto prepared cookie sheets.

♥ Bake at 400 degrees for 5 minutes or until lightly brown on bottom.

Yield: 24 cookies (Nutritional information per cookie)

Calories: 40
Percent Fat Calories: 7%
Carbohydrate: 9 grams
Protein: 0 grams

Total Fat: trace
Cholesterol: 0 mg
Dietary Fiber: 0 grams
Sodium: 62 mg

Menu Ideas: Good for breakfast, lunch or snacks.

Speedy
Sweets

(Delicious Date Cookies continued)

Incredible Cranberry Cookies: Follow recipe for Delicious Date Cookies exactly, except omit the chopped dates. Instead use ½ cup sweetened, dried cranberries (Craisins by Ocean Spray).

Yield: 24 cookies (Nutritional information per cookie)

Calories: 38
Percent Fat Calories: 8%
Carbohydrate: 8 grams
Protein: 0 grams

Total Fat: trace
Cholesterol: 0 mg
Dietary Fiber: 0 grams
Sodium: 62 mg

Radical Raisin Cookies: Follow recipe for Delicious Date Cookies exactly, except omit the chopped dates. Instead use ½ cup raisins.

Yield: 24 cookies (Nutritional information per cookie)

Calories: 40
Percent Fat Calories: 7%
Carbohydrate: 9 grams
Protein: 0 grams

Total Fat: trace
Cholesterol: 0 mg
Dietary Fiber: 0 grams
Sodium: 63 mg

Speedy Sweets

It's a wonderful thing when your best friend, your children's father, your lover and your husband are all the same person!

Dawn Hall

Total Time 9 minutes or less.

CITRUS SPICE COOKIES

Soft, fragrant and flavorful.
A good accompaniment with hot tea.

½ teaspoon ground cinnamon
¼ cup packed dark brown
   sugar
1 cup reduced-fat Bisquick
   baking mix

⅓ cup plus 1 tablespoon
   Sunny Delight citrus
   beverage (found in
   refrigerated juice section
   of store)

♥ Preheat oven to 400 degrees.

♥ Spray 2 cookie sheets with non-fat cooking spray. Set aside.

♥ Mix all ingredients together in a medium bowl with a spoon until well mixed.

♥ Drop by rounded teaspoonfuls onto prepared cookie sheets.

♥ Bake at 400 degrees for 4 minutes or until bottoms are lightly golden brown.

Yield: 24 cookies (Nutritional information per cookie)

Calories: 30
Percent Fat Calories: 10%
Carbohydrate: 6 grams
Protein: 0 grams

Total Fat: trace
Cholesterol: 0 mg
Dietary Fiber: 0 grams
Sodium: 62 mg

**Menu Ideas: Good with tea for
an afternoon snack or breakfast.**

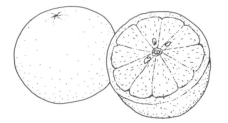

Budget
Friendly

Recipe

MAPLE COOKIES

*A delicious, flavorful cookie
that reminds me of Vermont.*

1   egg white
⅓ cup lite maple syrup
    (generic brands are fine)
1   cup reduced-fat Bisquick
    baking mix

¼ cup packed dark brown
    sugar
1   tablespoon powdered
    sugar

♥ Preheat oven to 400 degrees.

♥ Spray 2 cookie sheets with non-fat cooking spray. Set aside.

♥ Mix all ingredients, except powdered sugar, together with a
spatula in a medium bowl until well mixed.

♥ Drop by rounded teaspoonfuls onto prepared cookie sheets.

♥ Bake at 400 degrees for 4 minutes or until bottoms are
lightly golden brown.

♥ Sprinkle or sift top of cookies with powdered sugar.

Yield: 24 cookies (Nutritional information per cookie)

Calories: 36
Percent Fat Calories: 8%
Carbohydrate: 8 grams
Protein: 1 gram

Total Fat: trace
Cholesterol: 0 mg
Dietary Fiber: 0 grams
Sodium: 73 mg

**Menu Ideas: School lunches,
after school snack or after any meal.**

Speedy
Sweets

The best mirror is an old friend.

English Proverb

CREAMY RICE PUDDING

Budget
Friendly

Recipe

*This is a terrific way
to use leftover white rice.*

2 (1-ounce) boxes sugar-
free instant vanilla
pudding mix - dry - do
not make as directed on
box (I use Jell-O brand)
3½ cups cold skim milk

½ (8-ounce) container Cool
Whip Free - thawed
1 teaspoon almond
extract
1 cup raisins
2 cups cooked white rice

♥ With a whisk, in a medium-large bowl, briskly stir together dry pudding mixes and skim milk for 2 minutes.

♥ Stir in Cool Whip Free, almond extract, raisins and rice. Keep stirring until well mixed.

♥ Serve as is or keep chilled until ready to eat.

♥ If desired, sprinkle top very lightly with ground cinnamon before serving.

Yield: 14 (½-cup) servings

Calories: 120
Percent Fat Calories: 0%
Carbohydrate: 26 grams
Protein: 3 grams

Total Fat: 0 grams
Cholesterol: 1 mg
Dietary Fiber: 1 gram
Sodium: 115 mg

Menu Ideas: *Good anytime, anywhere.*

It seems like there is always leftover white rice when ordering Chinese takeout. Use the leftover cooked rice to make this delicious and creamy homestyle recipe without cooking at all!

Speedy
Sweets

Budget
Friendly
Recipe

BANANA-RAMA DESSERT

Smooth, creamy, rich and good for you.
(Who could ask for anything more?)

7 cinnamon graham
   crackers (4 sections
   equal 1 whole cracker)
2 (8-ounce) packages fat-
   free cream cheese -
   softened

6 packets Equal
1 (8-ounce) container Cool
   Whip Free - thawed
2 large bananas - cut into
   ¼-inch thick slices
1 teaspoon ground cinnamon

♥ Line a 9x13-inch pan with graham crackers. Make sure the cinnamon top of the crackers face down. You will need to break some crackers to fit.

♥ In a large bowl using a mixer on high speed, beat softened cream cheese with Equal for 2 minutes.

♥ Stir Cool Whip Free into the mixture until well blended. With a spatula, gently fold in banana slices.

♥ Spread cream mixture over graham crackers. Make sure bananas are not sticking out of cream mixture or they will turn dark in color.

♥ Sprinkle cinnamon evenly on top.

♥ Keep chilled until ready to serve.

Yield: 15 servings

Calories: 96
Percent Fat Calories: 7%
Carbohydrate: 16 grams
Protein: 5 grams

Total Fat: 1 gram
Cholesterol: 3 mg
Dietary Fiber: 1 gram
Sodium: 194 mg

Speedy
Sweets

***Menu Ideas:** A unique dessert to compliment a Mexican meal, such as Taco Salad.*

COOKIES AND CREAM
THREE-LAYER DESSERT

Budget Friendly Recipe

*The three layers are visually impressive.
This recipe was sent in by Dave Neiter, also known
as Dave Blade, Manager at Solid Rock Cafe; and
part-time D.J. on YES F.M. radio.*

1 (7¾-ounce) box Snackwell's chocolate sandwich cookies	2 (8-ounce) containers Cool Whip Free - thawed - divided
1 (8-ounce) Healthy Choice fat-free cream cheese - softened	2 (1.4-ounce) boxes chocolate fat-free, sugar-free instant pudding (Jell-O brand)
	3½ cups skim milk

♥ Put cookies in a 1-gallon zip-lock bag and crush with a rolling pin or hammer into small pieces. Set aside 2 tablespoons of the cookie crumbs.

♥ Mix cream cheese, 1½ containers of Cool Whip Free and remaining cookie crumbs in a medium bowl until well blended. Spread into a 9x13-inch glass pan.

♥ Make pudding as directed on box using 3½ cups milk. Spread prepared pudding over cookies and cream mixture.

♥ Spread remaining Cool Whip Free very thinly over pudding.

♥ Sprinkle reserved 2 tablespoons of cookie crumbs on top.

♥ Serve immediately or chill until ready to serve.

Yield: 20 servings

Calories: 107	Total Fat: 1 gram
Percent Fat Calories: 9%	Cholesterol: 1 mg
Carbohydrate: 20 grams	Dietary Fiber: 0 grams
Protein: 2 grams	Sodium: 318 mg

Menu Ideas: Good for any meal or potluck.

PEPPERMINT COOKIES

*These pretty peppermint cookies
will perk up any holiday gathering.*

COOKIES

2 peppermint candy canes
⅓ cup plus 1 tablespoon
  skim milk
1 cup reduced-fat Bisquick
  baking mix

¼ cup powdered sugar
½ teaspoon peppermint
  extract

GLAZE

2 tablespoons reduced-fat
  vanilla frosting (I use Betty
  Crocker Sweet Rewards)

1 drop mint extract

♥ Preheat oven to 400 degrees.

♥ Spray 2 cookie sheets with non-fat cooking spray. Set aside.

♥ Crush candy canes. Set aside one tablespoon of crushed candy cane for later. Use remaining candy for dough.

♥ In a medium bowl using a wooden spoon, mix remaining candy, milk, Bisquick, sugar and mint extract together until well mixed.

♥ Drop by rounded teaspoonfuls onto prepared cookie sheets and bake at 400 degrees for 4 minutes or until bottoms are golden brown.

♥ Microwave frosting for approximately 10 to 15 seconds, just enough to melt. Add mint extract to frosting and stir until well mixed.

♥ Drizzle frosting over cookies.

♥ Sprinkle tops with the reserved 1 tablespoon of crushed candy.

Yield: 24 cookies (Nutritional information per cookie)

Calories: 40
Percent Fat Calories: 10%
Carbohydrate: 8 grams
Protein: 1 gram

Total Fat: trace
Cholesterol: 0 mg
Dietary Fiber: 0 grams
Sodium: 64 mg

Menu Ideas: Great for holiday cookie trays.

Speedy Sweets

HONEY COOKIES

Budget Friendly Recipe

Converted from a high fat recipe.

½ cup honey
2 egg whites
½ cup applesauce
1 teaspoon baking soda

1 cup all-purpose flour
1½ teaspoons ground ginger
2 tablespoons Snackwell's
   vanilla frosting

♥ Preheat oven to 350 degrees.

♥ Spray cookie sheets with non-fat cooking spray. Set aside.

♥ Heat honey in a large microwave-safe bowl for 15 seconds.

♥ Stir in egg whites and applesauce with a spatula until well blended.

♥ Gradually stir in baking soda, flour and ginger.

♥ Drop by rounded teaspoonfuls onto prepared cookie sheets, about 1½ inches apart.

♥ Bake at 350 degrees for 10 to 12 minutes or until lightly golden brown.

♥ Microwave frosting in a small bowl 10 to 15 seconds or until melted. Lightly drizzle frosting over cookies with a spoon.

Yield: 48 cookies (Nutritional information per cookie)

Calories: 25
Percent Fat Calories: 0%
Carbohydrate: 6 grams
Protein: 0 grams

Total Fat: 0 grams
Cholesterol: 0 mg
Dietary Fiber: 0 grams
Sodium: 30 mg

Menu Ideas: Lunches or snacks.

Be generous with your love.

Budget Friendly Recipe

PISTACHIO COOKIES

The pretty "spring green" color make these
just right to serve during Easter or St. Patrick's Day.

⅓ cup plus 1 tablespoon water
1 cup reduced-fat Bisquick baking mix
1 (1-ounce) box pistachio fat-free, sugar-free instant pudding - dry - do not make as directed on box (Jell-O brand)

¼ cup plus 1 tablespoon sugar - divided
1 egg white
½ teaspoon almond extract

♥ Preheat oven to 350 degrees.

♥ Spray 2 cookie sheets with non-fat cooking spray. Set aside.

♥ Mix all ingredients except 1 tablespoon sugar together with a spoon until well mixed in a medium-sized bowl.

♥ Drop by rounded teaspoonfuls onto prepared cookie sheets. Evenly sprinkle cookies with remaining 1 tablespoon sugar.

♥ Bake for 8 minutes or until bottoms are lightly golden brown.

Yield: 24 cookies (Nutritional information per cookie)

Calories: 34
Percent Fat Calories: 9%
Carbohydrate: 7 grams
Protein: 1 gram

Total Fat: trace
Cholesterol: 0 mg
Dietary Fiber: 0 grams
Sodium: 109 mg

Menu Ideas: Spring, Easter or St. Patrick's Day buffet.

Speedy Sweets

Total Time: 15 minutes or less (per 2 dozen), 25 minutes (per 4 dozen).

CHEWY DATE COOKIES

Budget Friendly Recipe

Chewy, nutritious and delicious!

1 cup Lighter Bake butter and oil replacement (by Sunsweet, found in baking aisle)

1 cup powdered sugar
1½ cups all-purpose flour
½ cup chopped dates (I use Dole)

♥ Preheat oven to 375 degrees.

♥ Spray cookie sheets with non-fat cooking spray. Set aside.

♥ Mix Lighter Bake and sugar together until well blended in a medium-sized bowl.

♥ Gradually stir in flour. (Dough will become very stiff.)

♥ Stir in chopped dates.

♥ Drop by rounded teaspoonfuls onto prepared cookie sheets. Flatten dough by hand to ¼-inch to ⅓-inch thick.

♥ Bake at 375 degrees for 10 minutes.

Yield: 48 cookies (Nutritional information per cookie)

Calories: 39
Percent Fat Calories: 0%
Carbohydrate: 9 grams
Protein: 0 grams

Total Fat: 0 grams
Cholesterol: 0 mg
Dietary Fiber: 0 grams
Sodium: 2 mg

Menu Ideas: Lunches or snacks.

Raisin-Date Cookies: Make Date Cookie recipe exactly the same, but also add ¼ cup raisins to dough.

Yield: 54 cookies (Nutritional information per cookie)

Calories: 37
Percent Fat Calories: 0%
Carbohydrate: 9 grams
Protein: 0 grams

Total Fat: 0 grams
Cholesterol: 0 mg
Dietary Fiber: 0 grams
Sodium: 2 mg

(Chewy Date Cookies continued)

Cranberry-Date Cookies: Make Date Cookie recipe exactly the same, but also add ¼ cup chopped, dried cranberries.

Yield: 54 cookies (Nutritional information per cookie)

Calories: 36
Percent Fat Calories: 0%
Carbohydrate: 9 grams
Protein: 0 grams

Total Fat: 0 grams
Cholesterol: 0 mg
Dietary Fiber: 0 grams
Sodium: 2 mg

How much better our world would be if people would spend as much energy being concerned about the size of their hearts as they are the size of their wallets.

CHOCOLATE CHEWY COOKIES

Budget Friendly Recipe

Gloria Pitzer, the author of "The Recipe Detective", published a high fat version of this recipe and I converted it to an almost fat-free cookie. I give her all the credit for creating this delicious cookie, which she states reminds her of the kind Mrs. Field's used to have. Thank you Gloria for this wonderful cookie idea!

Gloria Pitzer has been a wonderful mentor and friend to me. If you are interested in her monthly newsletter her address is: Box 237, Marysville, Michigan 48040. The cost is $18.00 annually. Although they are not low-fat recipes, I'm sure you will agree with me that her recipes are mighty tasty!

1 (8-ounce) container Cool Whip Free
2 egg whites

1 (18.25-ounce) box reduced-fat chocolate cake mix - dry - do not make as directed on box (Sweet Rewards)
¼ cup powdered sugar

♥ Preheat oven to 350 degrees.

♥ Spray cookie sheets with non-fat cooking spray. Set aside.

♥ Beat Cool Whip Free until smooth, especially if frozen, then combine egg whites with Cool Whip Free in a medium-sized bowl.

♥ Mix dry cake mix into Cool Whip and egg white mixture. Stir until completely mixed.

♥ Dip rounded tablespoonfuls of cookie dough into powdered sugar.

♥ Place each cookie covered with powdered sugar onto prepared cookie sheet. Bake for 10 to 12 minutes until set but not brown.

♥ Cool a few minutes on cookie sheet, then transfer to waxed paper.

Yield: 58 cookies (Nutritional information per cookie)

Calories: 46
Percent Fat Calories: 16%
Carbohydrate: 9 grams
Protein: 0 grams

Total Fat: 1 gram
Cholesterol: 0 mg
Dietary Fiber: 0 grams
Sodium: 59 mg

Lemon Chewy Cookies: Make exactly the same but substitute lemon cake mix (Super Moist by Betty Crocker).

Yield: 58 cookies (Nutritional information per cookie)

Calories: 45
Percent Fat Calories: 14%
Carbohydrate: 9 grams
Protein: 0 grams

Total Fat: 1 gram
Cholesterol: 0 mg
Dietary Fiber: 0 grams
Sodium: 61 mg

Carrot Chewy Cookies: Make exactly the same but substitute carrot cake mix. (Super Moist by Betty Crocker).

Yield: 58 cookies (Nutritional information per cookie)

Calories: 46
Percent Fat Calories: 17%
Carbohydrate: 9 grams
Protein: 0 grams

Total Fat: 1 gram
Cholesterol: 0 mg
Dietary Fiber: 0 grams
Sodium: 60 mg

Speedy Sweets

DOUBLE CHOCOLATE
SOUR CREAM SNACK CAKE

Budget
Friendly

Recipe

Guaranteed to curb any chocolate sweet tooth!

1 (18.25-ounce) box
reduced-fat devil's food
cake mix - dry - do not
make as directed on box
(I use Betty Crocker
Sweet Rewards)

2 (4-ounce) containers Egg
Beaters (or 8 egg whites)
½ cup fat-free sour cream
¼ cup reduced-fat chocolate
frosting (I use Betty
Crocker Sweet Rewards)

♥ Preheat oven to 350 degrees.

♥ Spray an 11x17-inch jelly-roll pan with non-fat cooking spray.
Set aside.

♥ Mix all ingredients except frosting together in a medium
bowl with a spatula until well mixed.

♥ Spread into prepared pan.

♥ Bake at 350 degrees for 15 minutes.

♥ Microwave frosting for 15 to 25 seconds or until melted.
Drizzle over snack cake.

Yield: 20 squares (Nutritional information per square)

Calories: 130
Percent Fat Calories: 17%
Carbohydrate: 24 grams
Protein: 3 grams

Total Fat: 2 grams
Cholesterol: 0 mg
Dietary Fiber: 1 gram
Sodium: 233 mg

*Menu Ideas: Lunches, after school snacks,
potlucks or buffets.*

Double Chocolate Coconut Sour Cream Snack Cake:

Make Double Chocolate Sour Cream Snack Cake exactly the same except stir 1 teaspoon coconut extract into the batter. After spreading batter into prepared pan, sprinkle with ¼ cup shredded coconut. Bake at 350 degrees for 15 minutes. Drizzle melted chocolate frosting over baked coconut cake.

Yield: 20 squares (Nutritional information per square)

Calories: 137
Percent Fat Calories: 19%
Carbohydrate: 25 grams
Protein: 3 grams

Total Fat: 3 grams
Cholesterol: 0 mg
Dietary Fiber: 1 gram
Sodium: 236 mg

Chocolate Sour Cream Snack Cake:
Make Double Chocolate Sour Cream Snack Cake exactly the same, except do not use frosting. Instead sprinkle or sift 2 tablespoons powdered sugar over baked, cooled cake.

Yield: 20 squares (Nutritional information per square)

Calories: 120
Percent Fat Calories: 16%
Carbohydrate: 22 grams
Protein: 3 grams

Total Fat: 2 grams
Cholesterol: 0 mg
Dietary Fiber: 1 gram
Sodium: 224 mg

Speedy Sweets

PEANUT BUTTER CRUNCH BARS

Budget Friendly Recipe

This homemade version will save you oodles over the small packaged store brand! They're every bit as delicious! The blend of sweet, creamy peanut butter and the crunch make this a real hit for children! Great for school lunches.

8 cups Captain Crunch Peanut Butter Crunch cereal - divided

¼ cup Promise Ultra 70% less fat margarine
1 (10-ounce) bag marshmallows

♥ Spray a 9x13-inch pan with non-fat cooking spray. Set aside.

♥ Put 1 cup of the cereal in a zip-lock bag. Make sure the bag is securely closed, squeezing all the air out as you close. Crush the cereal. Set aside.

♥ In a large pan over low heat, melt Promise Ultra with marshmallows.

♥ Stir all of the cereal (crushed and not crushed) into marshmallow mixture.

♥ Spray hands with non-fat cooking spray. Press cereal mixture into prepared pan.

♥ Cool and cut into bars.

Yield: 16 bars

Calories: 137
Percent Fat Calories: 15%
Carbohydrate: 28 grams
Protein: 2 grams

Total Fat: 2 grams
Cholesterol: 0 mg
Dietary Fiber: 1 gram
Sodium: 155 mg

Menu Ideas: Great treat for lunches and snacks.

Speedy Sweets

Budget
Friendly
Recipe

BLACK FOREST TRIFLE

Kids Cookin'

*This is one of those desserts that
tastes too fattening to be non-fat!*

2 cups cold skim milk
1 (1.4-ounce) box chocolate
  sugar-free, fat-free instant
  pudding mix - dry - do not
  make as directed on box
1 (13.5-ounce) angel food
  cake (store bought) -
  torn into bite-size pieces

1 (21-ounce) can lite cherry
  pie filling
½ (8-ounce) container Cool
  Whip Free - thawed
2 tablespoons fat-free hot
  fudge (I use Smucker's)

♥ In a large bowl with a whisk, briskly mix cold milk with dry
  pudding for 2 minutes.

♥ With a spatula, stir pieces of torn angel food cake into
  pudding until cake pieces are saturated and have absorbed
  all of the pudding.

♥ Spread half of the cake mixture in the bottom of a large
  pretty glass serving bowl.

♥ Spread all of the pie filling over the cake mixture.

♥ Spread remaining cake mixture over cherry pie filling.

♥ Spread Cool Whip Free over cake mixture.

♥ Heat hot fudge in microwave on high for 10 seconds. Drizzle
  hot fudge over Cool Whip Free.

♥ Keep chilled until ready to serve.

Yield: 10 servings

Calories: 216
Percent Fat Calories: 4%
Carbohydrate: 48 grams
Protein: 4 grams

Total Fat: 1 gram
Cholesterol: 1 mg
Dietary Fiber: 1 gram
Sodium: 660 mg

Speedy
Sweets

***Menu Ideas: Chicken, fish or vegetarian-based entrées.
Great for showers, potlucks and special occasions.***

Butterscotch Rice Krispy Cookies

*This recipe was converted from a recipe
sent to us by Angie Auers of Maumee, Ohio.*

½ teaspoon cream of tartar	2 cups quick-cooking oatmeal (generic brands are fine)
1 cup applesauce	
1 cup Egg Beaters (or 8 egg whites)	
1 (18.25-ounce) box butter cake mix - dry - do not make as directed on box (I use Pillsbury Moist Supreme with pudding in the mix)	2 cups Rice Krispies (generic brands are fine)
	180 butterscotch chips (about ½ cup)

♥ Preheat oven to 375 degrees.

♥ Spray cookie sheets with non-fat cooking spray. Set aside.

♥ Mix cream of tartar, applesauce, Egg Beaters and dry cake mix together until well mixed.

♥ Stir in oatmeal and Rice Krispies.

♥ Drop by rounded teaspoonfuls onto prepared cookie sheets. Top each cookie with three butterscotch chips.

♥ Bake 10 minutes or until bottoms are golden brown.

Yield: 60 cookies (Nutritional information per cookie)

Calories: 59	Total Fat: 1 gram
Percent Fat Calories: 18%	Cholesterol: 0 mg
Carbohydrate: 11 grams	Dietary Fiber: 0 grams
Protein: 1 gram	Sodium: 71 mg

Menu Ideas: After school snack, or lunch box treats.

Budget
Friendly

Recipe

YUMMY TO YOUR TUMMY
JELLY ROLLS

My daughters, Whitney and Ashley,
created this yummy recipe!

10 teaspoons jelly (any flavor)   2 tablespoons sugar
1 (7.5-ounce) can Pillsbury
    biscuits

♥ Preheat oven to 450 degrees.

♥ Spray a 10-inch square pan with non-fat cooking spray. Set aside.

♥ With hands, flatten each biscuit into a 3-inch circle.

♥ Place individual biscuits on a flat surface.

♥ Put 1 teaspoon of jelly in middle of each biscuit. Fold together and stick a toothpick through the middle. (See diagram.) Place in prepared pan.

♥ Lightly sprinkle sugar on top and cook for 5 to 7 minutes.

Yield: 10 servings

Calories: 78
Percent Fat Calories: 9%
Carbohydrate: 17 grams
Protein: 1 gram

Total Fat: 1 gram
Cholesterol: 0 mg
Dietary Fiber: 0 grams
Sodium: 168 mg

Menu Ideas: Breakfast or an after school snack.

Speedy
Sweets

OATMEAL COOKIES

Budget
Friendly

Recipe

These crunchy cookies taste to me like a granola bar even though they are not shaped like one.

1 cup applesauce	¼ teaspoon nutmeg
1 cup packed brown sugar	4 cups rolled oats
1 teaspoon ground cinnamon	

♥ Preheat oven to 350 degrees.

♥ Spray cookie sheets with non-fat cooking spray. Set aside.

♥ Stir together applesauce, brown sugar, cinnamon and nutmeg until well blended in a medium-sized bowl.

♥ Gradually stir in oats until well blended.

♥ Drop by rounded teaspoonfuls onto prepared cookie sheets.

♥ Bake for 15 minutes or until lightly golden brown.

Yield: 48 cookies (Nutritional information per cookie)

Calories: 46	Total Fat: trace
Percent Fat Calories: 8%	Cholesterol: 0 mg
Carbohydrate: 10 grams	Dietary Fiber: 1 gram
Protein: 1 gram	Sodium: 2 mg

Menu Ideas: Lunches or snacks.

Cranberry Oatmeal Cookies: Stir in 1 cup chopped, dried cranberries (Ocean Spray) with the oatmeal.

Yield: 60 cookies (Nutritional information per cookie)

Calories: 42	Total Fat: trace
Percent Fat Calories: 8%	Cholesterol: 0 mg
Carbohydrate: 9 grams	Dietary Fiber: 1 gram
Protein: 1 gram	Sodium: 2 mg

Speedy
Sweets

(Oatmeal Cookies continued)

Raisin Oatmeal Cookies: Stir in 1 cup raisins with the oatmeal.

Yield: 60 cookies (Nutritional information per cookie)

Calories: 45
Percent Fat Calories: 7%
Carbohydrate: 10 grams
Protein: 1 gram

Total Fat: trace
Cholesterol: 0 mg
Dietary Fiber: 1 gram
Sodium: 2 mg

Oatmeal Date Cookies: Stir in 1 cup chopped dates with the oatmeal.

Yield: 60 cookies (Nutritional information per cookie)

Calories: 45
Percent Fat Calories: 7%
Carbohydrate: 10 grams
Protein: 1 gram

Total Fat: trace
Cholesterol: 0 mg
Dietary Fiber: 1 gram
Sodium: 2 mg

A cheerful, "hello" with a smile is a gift you give to brighten someone else's day.

SUGAR COOKIES
(SOFT DROP STYLE)

Budget
Friendly

Recipe

*This soft sugar cookie reminds our children of
an old family recipe titled "Madeline Cookies".
They are lightly sweetened.*

1½ cups powdered sugar
1 cup applesauce
2 egg whites
1½ teaspoons baking soda

1 teaspoon cream of tartar
2¼ cups all-purpose flour
1½ teaspoons almond
extract

♥ Preheat oven to 375 degrees.

♥ Spray cookie sheets with non-fat cooking spray. Set aside.

♥ Stir all ingredients until well mixed in a medium-sized bowl.

♥ Drop by rounded teaspoonfuls onto prepared cookie sheets.

♥ With hands, flatten dough on cookie sheet before baking.

♥ Bake at 375 degrees for 7 to 8 minutes.

♥ If desired, sprinkle with colored sugar before baking or frost after baking and once they are cooled. Frost with Snackwell's Frosting.

**This dough can be refrigerated
for weeks until ready to use.**

Yield: 48 cookies (Nutritional information per cookie)

Calories: 40
Percent Fat Calories: 0%
Carbohydrate: 9 grams
Protein: 1 gram

Total Fat: 0 grams
Cholesterol: 0 mg
Dietary Fiber: 0 grams
Sodium: 42 mg

Menu Ideas: *Good for packed lunches and snacks.*

Speedy
Sweets

Total Time: 20 minutes or less (derived mostly from cutting fruit).

FRESH PEACH DESSERT

A peachy-keen way to use fresh peaches!

1 (12-ounce) container Cool
  Whip Free - thawed
2 (8-ounce) packages
  fat-free cream cheese
½ cup sugar (or ½ cup
  Equal Spoonful)

8 large peaches - cut into
  ½-inch chunks
4 large bananas - cut into
  slices

♥ In a large bowl using a mixer on high speed, beat Cool Whip
  Free, cream cheese and sugar (or Equal Spoonful) together
  for 3 minutes.

♥ Gently stir in peaches and bananas.

♥ Serve as is or chill until ready to serve.

Yield: 12 (1-cup) servings

With sugar:
Calories: 203
Percent Fat Calories: 0%
Carbohydrate: 44 grams
Protein: 7 grams

Total Fat: 0 grams
Cholesterol: 3 mg
Dietary Fiber: 3 grams
Sodium: 199 mg

With Equal Spoonful:
Calories: 174
Percent Fat Calories: 0%
Carbohydrate: 35 grams
Protein: 7 grams

Total Fat: 0 grams
Cholesterol: 3 mg
Dietary Fiber: 3 grams
Sodium: 198 mg

Menu Ideas: Good as it is or on top of angel food cake.

Speedy
Sweets

MAPLE SNACK CAKE

Budget
Friendly

Recipe

*Great served warm with a dab of Cool Whip
Free. Also great at room temperature for packed lunches.*

³/₄ cup lite maple syrup
2 tablespoons applesauce
8 egg whites (or 1 cup Egg
  Beaters)
1 (18.25-ounce) box reduced-
  fat yellow cake mix - do not
  make as directed on box
  (I use Betty Crocker
  Sweet Rewards)

⅓ cup water
1 (8-ounce) container Cool
  Whip Free (or 2 tablespoons
  powdered sugar)

♥ Preheat oven to 350 degrees.

♥ Spray an 11x17-inch jelly-roll pan with non-fat cooking spray.
  Set aside.

♥ Briskly mix all ingredients except Cool Whip Free with whisk
  in a medium bowl for 1 minute.

♥ Pour into prepared pan.

♥ Bake at 350 degrees for 16 minutes or until a toothpick
  inserted in center comes out clean.

♥ To serve warm: Serve with a dab (about 2 tablespoons per
  serving) of Cool Whip Free.

To serve at room temperature: Once completely cooled,
sprinkle or sift 2 tablespoons powdered sugar on top of
entire cake.

Yield: 24 servings

With Cool Whip Free:
Calories: 116
Percent Fat Calories: 4%
Carbohydrate: 25 grams
Protein: 2 grams

Total Fat: 1 gram
Cholesterol: 0 mg
Dietary Fiber: 0 grams
Sodium: 190 mg

(Maple Snack Cake continued)

<u>With powdered sugar:</u>

Calories: 103

Percent Fat Calories: 4%

Carbohydrate: 23 grams

Protein: 2 grams

Total Fat: 1 gram

Cholesterol: 0 mg

Dietary Fiber: 0 grams

Sodium: 185 mg

Menu Ideas: A dessert or snack.

Total Time: 20 minutes.

CHOCOLATE AND BANANA CREAM LAYERED DESSERT

Budget Friendly Recipe

Simple and sweet.

45 chocolate reduced-fat Nabisco Nilla wafers – divided

4 (0.9-ounce) boxes sugar-free instant banana cream pudding - dry - do not make as directed on box - divided

7½ cups skim milk - divided

3 cups Cool Whip Free (one 8-ounce container) - divided

2 (0.9-ounce) boxes sugar free instant chocolate pudding - dry - do not make as directed on box

♥ In the bottom of a 9x13-inch glass pan, arrange 35 chocolate wafers. Set aside.

♥ Mix 2 boxes of banana cream pudding mix with 2½ cups skim milk. Once smooth and creamy, stir in 1 cup Cool Whip Free. Spread over wafers. Set aside.

♥ Mix dry chocolate pudding mix with 2½ cups skim milk until smooth and creamy. Stir 1 cup Cool Whip Free into pudding. Spread over banana cream pudding.

♥ Mix remaining 2 boxes of banana cream pudding with 2½ cups milk until smooth and creamy. Stir in 1 cup Cool Whip Free. Spread over chocolate pudding.

♥ Crush remaining 10 wafers. Sprinkle on top.

♥ Serve immediately or chill until ready to serve.

Yield: 15 servings

Calories: 152
Percent Fat Calories: 9%
Carbohydrate: 29 grams
Protein: 5 grams

Total Fat: 2 grams
Cholesterol: 2 mg
Dietary Fiber: 0 grams
Sodium: 603 mg

Menu Ideas: *Good for large gatherings, such as potlucks.*

Speedy Sweets

Budget
Friendly

CHRISTMAS TREE CINNAMON ROLLS

Recipe

*A creative way to serve an old
time favorite. As pretty as it is yummy.*

2 (10-ounce) cans pizza
dough (I use Pillsbury)
2 tablespoons fat-free
Ultra Promise margarine
½ cup sugar
2 teaspoons ground
cinnamon

⅓ cup Snackwell's vanilla
frosting
Green colored sugar
(Betty Crocker, found in
baking aisle.) - optional
11 maraschino cherries -
halved - optional

♥ Preheat oven 350 degrees.

♥ Spray a cookie sheet with non-fat cooking spray. Set aside.

♥ Unroll dough and press each piece into an 11x17-inch rectangle.
Spread a tablespoon of margarine on each rectangle.

♥ Mix sugar and cinnamon together. Sprinkle mixture evenly
over rectangles.

♥ Roll up rectangles jelly-roll style, starting with a long side.
Pinch dough to seal edge.

♥ Cut each roll into 11 slices (for a total of 22 slices).

♥ **To make a Christmas tree:** Place slices as diagram dis-
plays - with sides touching. **To make a wreath:** make into a
circle with 8 slices inside and 14 outside.

♥ Bake at 350 degrees for 18 to 20 minutes or until golden brown.

♥ Invert Christmas wreath or tree onto a large plate.

♥ Microwave frosting until warm. Drizzle frosting over the top.

♥ Sprinkle lightly with green colored sugar.

♥ Decorate with cherry halves.

O
OO
OOO
OOOO
OOOOO
OOOOOO
O

Speedy Sweets

Yield: 11 servings (2 rolls per serving)

Calories: 185	Total Fat: 2 grams
Percent Fat Calories: 11%	Cholesterol: 0 mg
Carbohydrate: 37 grams	Dietary Fiber: 1 gram
Protein: 4 grams	Sodium: 293 mg

Menu Ideas: Breakfast - orange juice and a fruit cup.

APPLE PAN DOWDY

Budget
Friendly

Recipe

*At a book signing in Fort Wayne, Indiana,
someone gave me the name and idea for this recipe.*

1 (21-ounce) can apple pie filling	1 tablespoon ground cinnamon
1 (7.5-ounce) can buttermilk biscuits (I use Pillsbury)	1 tablespoon Butter Buds Sprinkles - dry
¼ cup packed dark brown sugar	½ teaspoon ground cloves

♥ Preheat oven to 425 degrees.

♥ Spray a 9-inch square baking pan with non-fat cooking spray.

♥ Spread pie filling on bottom of pan.

♥ Arrange biscuits on top of pie filling.

♥ Mix brown sugar, cinnamon, Butter Buds and ground cloves together until well mixed. Sprinkle seasonings on top of biscuits.

♥ Bake at 425 degrees for 10 minutes. Take pan out of oven, turn biscuits over and return to oven for another 5 to 8 minutes.

Yield: 9 servings

Calories: 151	Total Fat: 1 gram
Percent Fat Calories: 6%	Cholesterol: 0 mg
Carbohydrate: 35 grams	Dietary Fiber: 1 gram
Protein: 2 grams	Sodium: 256 mg

Menu Ideas: Breakfast, brunch or dessert.

Speedy
Sweets

BROWNIE PIZZA

*Wonderful idea for birthday
parties instead of cake!*

1 (10.25-ounce) package
   fudge brownie mix - dry -
   do not make as directed
   on box (I use Betty
   Crocker)
3 tablespoons applesauce
2 egg whites

2 tablespoons water
¼ cup fat-free hot fudge
   sundae topping
   (Smucker's)
2 tablespoons Hershey's
   holiday bits or your
   favorite topping.

♥ Preheat oven to 350 degrees.

♥ Spray an 8-inch cake pan with non-fat cooking spray. Set
   aside.

♥ Mix brownie mix, applesauce, egg whites and water together
   with a spoon for about 1 minute in a medium-sized bowl.

♥ Spread mixture in prepared cake pan.

♥ Bake at 350 degrees for 20 minutes.

♥ Remove cake from pan.

♥ Frost with fat-free hot fudge while still warm.

♥ Sprinkle with holiday bits. Cut into 8 pizza slices.

Yield: 8 servings

Calories: 198
Percent Fat Calories: 22%
Carbohydrate: 37 grams
Protein: 4 grams

Total Fat: 5 grams
Cholesterol: 1 mg
Dietary Fiber: 2 grams
Sodium: 179 mg

Speedy
Sweets

Menu Ideas: *Any children's celebration.*

Total Time: 40 minutes or less (including baking and cooling time).

Four-Layer Lemon Cake

Budget
Friendly

Recipe

Light, lemony and luscious!

CAKE

1 (3-ounce) box lemon gelatin - dry - do not make as directed on box (I use Jell-O brand)
1 cup hot water
1 (18.25-ounce) box reduced-fat yellow cake mix - dry (do not make as directed on box (Betty Crocker Sweet Rewards)

½ cup Smucker's Baking Healthy Shortening and Oil Replacement
6 egg whites
1 (15.75-ounce) can lemon pie filling (I use Thank You brand)

GLAZE - OPTIONAL (NOT NEEDED, BUT IT DOES ADD AN EXTRA SPECIAL TOUCH AND PRETTY APPEARANCE.)

⅓ cup powdered sugar

1 tablespoon bottled lemon juice

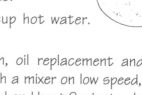

♥ Preheat oven to 350 degrees.

♥ Spray four 8-inch cake pans with non-fat cooking spray. Set aside.

♥ Dissolve lemon gelatin into 1 cup hot water. Stir until completely dissolved.

♥ Combine cake, dissolved gelatin, oil replacement and egg whites in a large mixing bowl, with a mixer on low speed, until moistened. Increase to high speed and beat 2 minutes longer.

♥ Divide cake batter evenly into prepared pans.

♥ Bake at 350 degrees for 20 to 25 minutes. Cake is done when a toothpick inserted in center comes out clean. (Note: The cakes baking on the top rack in the oven may be done first. If so, remove top cakes. Move bottom rack cakes up to top rack and continue cooking until done.)

♥ Let cakes cool 10 minutes. Remove from pans.

(Four-Layer Lemon Cake continued)

♥ Divide and spread lemon pie filling evenly over the top of each cake. Stack cake layers on top of each other.

♥ To make glaze, mix together with a spoon powdered sugar and lemon juice until well mixed. Microwave on high for 30 seconds. Drizzle over cake, letting glaze run down the sides.

Yield: 16 servings

With glaze:

Calories: 268	Total Fat: 3 grams
Percent Fat Calories: 9%	Cholesterol: 37 mg
Carbohydrate: 58 grams	Dietary Fiber: 0 grams
Protein: 5 grams	Sodium: 275 mg

Without glaze:

Calories: 258	Total Fat: 3 grams
Percent Fat Calories: 9%	Cholesterol: 37 mg
Carbohydrate: 55 grams	Dietary Fiber: 0 grams
Protein: 5 grams	Sodium: 275 mg

Menu Ideas: Special occasions.

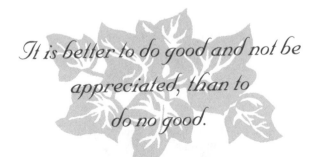

It is better to do good and not be appreciated, than to do no good.

Total Time: 25 minutes or less.

CITRUS SPICE SNACK CAKE

*Delicious warm. The wonderful
aroma entices everybody!*

3½ cups reduced-fat
   Bisquick baking mix
1½ cups orange juice
½ cup plus ⅔ cup packed
   brown sugar - divided

4 egg whites
2 tablespoons applesauce
2 teaspoons ground
   cinnamon - divided

♥ Preheat oven to 375 degrees.

♥ Spray an 11x17-inch jelly-roll pan with non-fat cooking spray.
Set aside.

♥ Mix all ingredients, except ⅔ cup brown sugar and one
teaspoon ground cinnamon, together until well blended in a
medium-sized bowl.

♥ Spread in prepared pan.

♥ Mix remaining ⅔ cup brown sugar and 1 teaspoon ground
cinnamon together and sprinkle over cake.

♥ Bake 15 to 18 minutes or until golden brown.

Yield: 20 servings

Calories: 141
Percent Fat Calories: 9%
Carbohydrate: 30 grams
Protein: 2 grams

Total Fat: 1 gram
Cholesterol: 0 mg
Dietary Fiber: 0 grams
Sodium: 260 mg

Menu Ideas: Good for brunch, breakfast or a snack.

COOKIES AND CREAM BROWNIES

These brownies are super rich!
A little serving goes a long way.

1 (16-ounce) package
  brownie mix - dry - do not
  make as directed on box
3 tablespoons applesauce
5 egg whites - divided
3 tablespoons water

12 reduced-fat Oreo's -
   crushed - divided
1 (8-ounce) package fat-free
   cream cheese - softened
¼ cup sugar

♥ Preheat oven to 350 degrees.

♥ Spray a 9x13-inch nonstick pan with non-fat cooking spray.
  Set aside.

♥ With a fork, mix brownie mix, applesauce, 2 egg whites and
  water together until well blended in a medium-sized bowl.
  Stir in three-fourths of the crushed Oreo's.

♥ Spread in prepared pan.

♥ With a mixer, beat 3 egg whites, cream cheese and sugar
  together until smooth. Spoon cream cheese mixture over
  batter. Cut through batter with a knife to swirl. Sprinkle
  with remaining crushed Oreo's.

♥ Bake at 350 degrees for 25 minutes or until a toothpick
  inserted in center comes out clean.

Yield: 20 servings

Calories: 150
Percent Fat Calories: 19%
Carbohydrate: 27 grams
Protein: 4 grams

Total Fat: 3 grams
Cholesterol: 4 mg
Dietary Fiber: 0 grams
Sodium: 266 mg

Menu Ideas: Great for picnics.

Speedy
Sweets

Total Time: 25 minutes.

LEMON BREAKFAST BAKE

This is so yummy, you may not want to serve it just for breakfast. Also good for after school snacks!

1 (7.5-ounce) can buttermilk biscuits (I use Pillsbury)
1 (8-ounce) package fat-free cream cheese

½ cup sugar
2 egg whites
½ teaspoon lemon extract

♥ Preheat oven to 375 degrees.

♥ Spray a 9x13-inch baking dish with non-fat cooking spray.

♥ With hands, flatten biscuits into bottom of prepared dish, forming it together to cover entire dish.

♥ With a mixer, beat cream cheese, sugar, egg whites and lemon extract together until well mixed.

♥ Spoon filling over top of biscuit layer and bake at 375 degrees for 20 minutes.

Yield: 20 servings

Calories: 57
Percent Fat Calories: 6%
Carbohydrate: 11 grams
Protein: 3 grams

Total Fat: trace
Cholesterol: 1 mg
Dietary Fiber: 0 grams
Sodium: 143 mg

Menu Ideas: Breakfast and brunches.

What soap is for the body, tears are for the soul.

Jewish Proverbs

TURTLE CAKE

*A special three-layer cake
for a special occasion.*

1⅓ cups water
½ cup applesauce
6 egg whites
1 (18.25-ounce) box
chocolate fudge super
moist cake mix - dry (I use
Betty Crocker) - do not
make as directed on box

6 tablespoons fat-free
caramel sundae topping
2 ounces Cool Whip Free
(¼ of an 8-ounce container)
2 tablespoons finely
chopped pecans

♥ Preheat oven to 350 degrees.

♥ Spray three 8-inch round cake pans with non-fat cooking spray. Set aside.

♥ Mix water, applesauce, egg whites and dry cake mix together with a whisk for 1 minute in a medium-sized bowl.

♥ Bake in prepared pans for 16 to 18 minutes or until a toothpick inserted in center comes out clean.

♥ Let cool for 7 minutes.

♥ Remove cakes one at a time. Spread 2 tablespoons of caramel topping on top of each of the three layers. Stack the layers.

♥ Serve immediately or chill until ready to serve.

♥ Just before servings, frost top layer with Cool Whip Free. Sprinkle with finely chopped pecans.

Yield: 12 servings

Calories: 240
Percent Fat Calories: 18%
Carbohydrate: 45 grams
Protein: 4 grams

Total Fat: 5 grams
Cholesterol: 0 mg
Dietary Fiber: 1 gram
Sodium: 322 mg

Menu Ideas: This would compliment any special meal.

Speedy
Sweets

Cappuccino Cake
with Cappuccino Frosting

Whether you make three single layer cakes or one impressive looking three-layer cake, this recipe tastes delicious! It's rich, smooth and moist!

Cake

1 (18.25-ounce) package devil's food super moist cake mix - dry - do not make as directed on box (I use Betty Crocker)

1⅓ cups water

4 egg whites
1 tablespoon instant coffee
1 teaspoon ground cinnamon
½ cup applesauce

Cappuccino Frosting

1 (16-ounce) container reduced-fat milk chocolate frosting (I use Betty Crocker Sweet Rewards)

1 tablespoon instant coffee
1¼ teaspoons ground cinnamon

♥ Preheat oven to 350 degrees.

♥ Spray three 8-inch round cake pans with non-fat cooking spray. Set aside.

♥ Beat cake mix, water, egg whites, instant coffee, cinnamon and applesauce on low speed for 1 minute, scraping bowl constantly. (Or stir by hand for 2 minutes.) Divide batter evenly into prepared pans.

♥ Bake at 350 degrees for 15 to 20 minutes or until a toothpick inserted in center comes out clean.

♥ In the meantime, while cakes are baking you can make the frosting. With a spatula, combine frosting, instant coffee and cinnamon in a bowl until well blended.

(Cappuccino Cake with Cappuccino Frosting continued)

♥ Cool cakes for 10 minutes in pan.

♥ To make 3 small cakes: Either remove cakes from pans or keep in pans. Divide frosting evenly among cakes and carefully frost tops, even though cakes are still warm. Sprinkle lightly with additional ground cinnamon, if desired. Cut each cake into 6 pieces.

Yield: 18 servings

Calories: 218
Percent Fat Calories: 20%
Carbohydrate: 41 grams
Protein: 3 grams

Total Fat: 5 grams
Cholesterol: 0 mg
Dietary Fiber: 1 gram
Sodium: 290 mg

To make one 3-layer cake: The one three layer cake will take more time to cool before it can be frosted and stacked. Remove cakes from pans and cool completely before frosting. Frost tops of each cake and stack. Do not frost sides. Sprinkle lightly with additional ground cinnamon, if desired.

Yield: 12 servings

Calories: 327
Percent Fat Calories: 20%
Carbohydrate: 62 grams
Protein: 4 grams

Total Fat: 7 grams
Cholesterol: 0 mg
Dietary Fiber: 2 grams
Sodium: 434 mg

Cappuccino Snack Cake: Prepare cake exactly as directed and bake in three 9-inch square pans. Do not frost. Instead, sprinkle lightly with cinnamon, if desired. Cut each pan into 9 squares.

Yield: 27 servings

Calories: 83
Percent Fat Calories: 19%
Carbohydrate: 15 grams
Protein: 1 gram

Total Fat: 2 grams
Cholesterol: 0 mg
Dietary Fiber: 1 gram
Sodium: 154 mg

BLACK FOREST CAKE

Budget Friendly Recipe

Chocolate and cherries never had it so good.

1 (18.25-ounce) box devil's food reduced-fat cake mix- do not make as directed on box - (I use Betty Crocker Sweet Rewards)

1⅓ cups water

2 tablespoons applesauce

6 egg whites

1 (21-ounce) can cherry pie filling

2 tablespoons fat-free chocolate cherries jubilee syrup (Hershey's) or fat-free chocolate syrup

♥ Preheat oven to 350 degrees.

♥ Spray three 8-inch round cake pans with non-fat cooking spray. Set aside.

♥ Beat cake mix, water, applesauce and egg whites with a wire whisk (or large spoon) for 1 minute in a medium-sized bowl.

♥ Pour into prepared pans.

♥ Bake at 350 degrees for 16 to 18 minutes or until a toothpick inserted in center comes out clean.

♥ Three small individual cakes: Leave cakes in pan. Divide and spread cherry pie filling on top of the 3 cakes. Drizzle syrup on top. Cut each cake into 8 pieces.

Yield: 24 servings

Calories: 125
Percent Fat Calories: 13%
Carbohydrate: 25 grams
Protein: 2 grams

Total Fat: 2 grams
Cholesterol: 0 mg
Dietary Fiber: 1 gram
Sodium: 184 mg

Total Time: 20 minutes.

Menu Ideas: Dessert, potlucks or Bible studies.

Speedy Sweets

One large three-layer cake: Cool cakes 10 minutes in pan. Remove cakes (one at a time) from pans. Spread one-third of pie filling over each layer. Stack cakes three layers high. Drizzle syrup over top layer and let syrup run down the sides of the cake. Very impressive to look at!

Yield: 12 servings

Calories: 249
Percent Fat Calories: 13%
Carbohydrate: 51 grams
Protein: 4 grams

Total Fat: 4 grams
Cholesterol: 0 mg
Dietary Fiber: 2 grams
Sodium: 368 mg

Menu Ideas: Special dinners or events.

In matters of style, swim with the current; in matters of principle, stand like a rock.

Thomas Jefferson

Speedy
Sweets

MARASCHINO CHERRY CAKE
WITH CREAM SAUCE

Budget
Friendly

Recipe

*The thick, rich, cream sauce makes this dessert
very special. My mouth waters as I watch the special
sauce ooze down the sides of each serving.*

CAKE

1 (10-ounce) jar
   maraschino cherries
2 tablespoons applesauce
6 egg whites

1 (18.25-ounce) box
  reduced-fat yellow cake
  mix - dry - do not make
  as directed on box (I use
  Betty Crocker Sweet
  Rewards)

CREAM SAUCE

1 pint fat-free half & half
  (I use Land O Lakes)

1 (4.6-ounce) box vanilla
  cook and serve pudding
  and pie filling mix - dry -
  do not make as directed
  on box (I use Jell-O brand)

♥ Preheat oven to 350 degrees.

♥ Spray three 8-inch round cake pans with non-fat cooking
  spray. Set aside.

♥ Drain juice from maraschino cherries into a measuring cup.
  Add enough water to the maraschino cherry juice to measure 1 cup.

♥ Set maraschino cherries aside.

♥ In a medium bowl, mix together juice/water mixture, applesauce and egg whites until well blended. Stir in cake mix.
  Scraping bowl constantly, stir for 2 minutes.

♥ Divide the maraschino cherries evenly among the bottom of
  the prepared pans.

♥ Pour batter over cherries in pans.

(Maraschino Cherry Cake continued)

♥ Bake at 350 degrees for 20 to 25 minutes. (Cakes are done when a toothpick inserted in center comes out clean.)

♥ Meantime, while cakes are baking, prepare cream sauce. In a 2-quart nonstick saucepan, cook the half & half with the pudding mix over medium heat, stirring constantly, until mixture comes to a full boil.

♥ Remove from heat. Let cream mixture sit until cakes are finished baking.

♥ Once cakes are completely baked, carefully cut (steak knives work well) each cake into 8 pieces. Place each serving on an individual dessert plate.

♥ Put a dab of the warm cream sauce on top of each serving. Allow the sauce to ooze down the sides.

♥ Serve warm.

Yield: 24 servings

Calories: 132	Total Fat: 1 gram
Percent Fat Calories: 3%	Cholesterol: 0 mg
Carbohydrate: 30 grams	Dietary Fiber: 0 grams
Protein: 3 grams	Sodium: 208 mg

Menu Ideas: For special occasions, teas, Bible studies, coffees, etc.

Total Time: 30 minutes or less.

PUMPKIN PARTY DESSERT

This recipe was submitted by Angie Auers of Maumee, Ohio. Her version had 10 ingredients and took 45 minutes to bake. My fast and easy version of her recipe is great! With 40 servings, it's good for parties.

1 (8-ounce) carton Egg Beaters (or 8 egg whites)
1 cup skim milk
1 (30-ounce) can pumpkin pie mix (I use Libby's brand)

2 (18.25-ounce) boxes butter cake mix - dry - do not make as directed on box (I use Pillsbury Moist Supreme brand with pudding in the mix)
3 tablespoons Butter Buds Sprinkles
1 cup warm water

♥ Preheat oven to 350 degrees.

♥ Spray two 11x17-inch jelly-roll pans with non-fat cooking spray. Set aside.

♥ Mix Egg Beaters, milk and pumpkin pie mix together until well blended in a medium-sized bowl.

♥ Divide and spread mixture evenly on the bottom of prepared jelly-roll pans.

♥ Sprinkle one box of dry cake mix on top of each jelly-roll pan of prepared pumpkin mixture.

♥ Dissolve Butter Buds into warm water.

♥ Drizzle (or spray) Butter Buds mixture over cake mix. (Make sure you evenly distribute the Butter Buds mixture over both cakes!) Note: Use a spray bottle to spray Butter Buds mixture on the cake or drizzle using a water bottle for more control.

♥ Bake in oven at 350 degrees for 25 minutes.

♥ Best served warm with a dab of Cool Whip Free. However, it is still yummy at room temperature or served chilled.

(Pumpkin Party Dessert continued)

Yield: 40 servings. Cut each dessert pan into 20 squares.

Calories: 131
Percent Fat Calories: 12%
Carbohydrate: 27 grams
Protein: 2 grams

Total Fat: 2 grams
Cholesterol: 0 mg
Dietary Fiber: 1 gram
Sodium: 231 mg

**Menu Ideas: Pork Tenderloin, lean ham, chicken or turkey.
Great for groups of 15 or more (usually people ask for
seconds because it is so good.)**

Total Time: 30 minutes or less.

Chocolate Brownie Four-Layer Cake

*Rich and heavy . . . a little serving
goes a long way!*

1 (21.3-ounce) box dark
chocolate supreme
brownie mix with syrup
pouch (I use Betty
Crocker) dry - do not
make as directed on
package

¼ cup water

½ cup applesauce

6 egg whites

1 (12-ounce) container Cool
Whip Free - thawed

1 (1.4-ounce) box chocolate
fat-free, sugar-free
instant pudding mix - dry
- do not make as directed
on package (I use Jell-O
brand)

2 tablespoons Hershey's
lite chocolate syrup

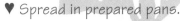

♥ Preheat oven to 350 degrees.

♥ Spray four 8-inch round cake pans with non-fat cooking spray. Set aside.

♥ Stir brownie mix and contents of syrup pouch, water, applesauce and egg whites together in a large bowl for 1 minute or until well mixed.

♥ Spread in prepared pans.

♥ Bake for 17 to 20 minutes or until a toothpick inserted 2 inches from side of pan comes out almost clean.

♥ In the meantime, while brownies are baking, make the cream filling. Stir Cool Whip Free and dry pudding mix together for 2 minutes or until well blended. Refrigerate until ready to use.

♥ Once brownies are baked, put in freezer for 5 minutes to cool more quickly.

♥ Frost top of brownie cakes with chocolate cream mixture.

♥ Stack the frosted layers on top of each other into a 4-layer cake.

♥ Drizzle with chocolate syrup.

♥ Keep refrigerated until ready to serve.

Speedy Sweets

(Chocolate Brownie Four-Layer Cake continued)

Yield: 14 servings

Calories: 239
Percent Fat Calories: 8%
Carbohydrate: 49 grams
Protein: 3 grams

Total Fat: 2 grams
Cholesterol: 0 mg
Dietary Fiber: 0 grams
Sodium: 299 mg

**Menu Ideas: Because it is so heavy and filling, this
dessert is best served by itself (with coffee at a Bible
study or at a "tea"). However, it also is good after a light
meal such as baked fish, soup or salad.**

Speedy Sweets

*If you're not generous with
what little you have, chances are you're not
going to be generous when you have more.*

CHOCOLATE BREAD PUDDING

Budget
Friendly

Recipe

An all around great dessert!

1 (14-ounce) can Eagle fat-free sweetened condensed milk	6 egg whites (or ¾ cup Egg Beaters)
1¼ cups Hershey's fat-free chocolate syrup	12 slices fat-free bread, cut into cubes (leave crust on)
1 cup skim milk	½ cup chocolate chips
	½ (8-ounce) container Cool Whip Free - optional

♥ Preheat oven to 350 degrees.

♥ Spray an 11x17-inch jelly-roll pan with non-fat cooking spray. Set aside.

♥ In a large bowl, mix condensed milk, chocolate syrup, milk and egg whites until well blended.

♥ Stir in bread cubes.

♥ Spread into prepared pan.

♥ Sprinkle with chocolate chips.

♥ Bake at 350 degrees for 20 minutes or until a knife inserted in the center comes out clean.

♥ Serve warm, with a dab of Cool Whip Free, if desired. (Also good at room temperature or chilled).

Yield: 15 servings

Calories: 244	Total Fat: 2 grams
Percent Fat Calories: 6%	Cholesterol: 2 mg
Carbohydrate: 50 grams	Dietary Fiber: 1 gram
Protein: 6 grams	Sodium: 204 mg

Menu Ideas: Potlucks, buffets and special occasions.

Use the exact recipe for Chocolate Bread Pudding then top with the following for additional delicious desserts!

Black Forest Bread Pudding: After pudding is baked, top with one 21-ounce can of cherry pie filling. Drizzle each serving with 1 tablespoon lite chocolate syrup. (I use Hershey's).

Yield: 15 servings

Calories: 314
Percent Fat Calories: 5%
Carbohydrate: 67 grams
Protein: 7 grams

Total Fat: 2 grams
Cholesterol: 2 mg
Dietary Fiber: 1 gram
Sodium: 231 mg

Chocolate Monkey Bread Pudding: After baking and just before serving, cut 2 bananas into ¼-inch thick slices. Arrange slices on bread pudding. Dab each serving with 2 tablespoons Cool Whip Free. Drizzle 1 tablespoon of lite chocolate syrup over each serving. (I use Hershey's).

Yield: 15 servings

Calories: 298
Percent Fat Calories: 6%
Carbohydrate: 62 grams
Protein: 7 grams

Total Fat: 2 grams
Cholesterol: 2 mg
Dietary Fiber: 2 grams
Sodium: 233 mg

Grasshopper Bread Pudding: After pudding is baked, top each serving with a ¼-cup scoop of fat-free chocolate chip mint ice cream (I use Breyer's). Drizzle each serving with 1 tablespoon lite chocolate syrup. (I use Hershey's).

Yield: 15 servings

Calories: 344
Percent Fat Calories: 5%
Carbohydrate: 72 grams
Protein: 8 grams

Total Fat: 2 grams
Cholesterol: 4 mg
Dietary Fiber: 1 gram
Sodium: 268 mg

Turtle Bread Pudding: After pudding is baked, spread one cup of fat-free caramel topping over entire pan. Top each serving with 2 tablespoons Cool Whip Free and 1 teaspoon finely chopped pecans.

Yield: 15 servings

Calories: 344
Percent Fat Calories: 9%
Carbohydrate: 70 grams
Protein: 7 grams

Total Fat: 3 grams
Cholesterol: 2 mg
Dietary Fiber: 1 gram
Sodium: 268 mg

Speedy Sweets

Notes

_____

_____

_____

_____

_____

_____

_____

_____

_____

_____

_____

_____

_____

_____

_____

_____

_____

_____

_____

_____

_____

Crockpot Creations

CLAM CHOWDER

There's NO WAY anyone would ever know this is low fat if you didn't tell them! It's super thick, rich and creamy.

3 (10.75-ounce) cans Campbell's 98% fat-free cream of celery soup

2 (6.5-ounce) cans chopped clams - do not drain

1 (1-pound) bag frozen fat-free shredded hash brown potatoes

½ cup frozen chopped onion

1 pint fat-free half & half

♥ Spray a crockpot with non-fat cooking spray.

♥ Put all ingredients in crockpot. Stir until well mixed.

♥ Cover.

♥ Cook on low for 8 to 9 hours.

Yield: 11 (1-cup) servings

Calories: 130
Percent Fat Calories: 15%
Carbohydrate: 21 grams
Protein: 8 grams

Total Fat: 2 grams
Cholesterol: 15 mg
Dietary Fiber: 1 gram
Sodium: 782 mg

Menu Ideas: Oyster crackers and Spring Salad (page 120 of "Busy People's Low-Fat Cookbook".)

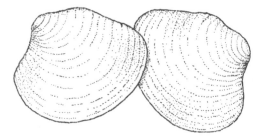

CREAM OF BROCCOLI
AND MUSHROOM SOUP

*This thick, rich soup will stick to your bones,
but not your hips, thighs or arteries.*

8 ounces fresh mushrooms,
   sliced
2 (1-pound) bags frozen
   broccoli stems and pieces
3 (10.75-ounce) cans
   Campbell's 98% fat-free
   cream of broccoli soup

½ teaspoon dried thyme,
   crushed
3 bay leaves
1 pint fat-free half & half
4 ounces extra lean,
   smoked ham - cut into
   tiny pieces

♥ Put all ingredients into a crockpot. Mix well. Cover.

♥ Cook on low for 8 to 9 hours or on high for 3½ to 4 hours.

♥ Remove bay leaves before eating.

Yield: 12 (1-cup) servings

Calories: 114
Percent Fat Calories: 19%
Carbohydrate: 17 grams
Protein: 9 grams

Total Fat: 3 grams
Cholesterol: 11 mg
Dietary Fiber: 3 grams
Sodium: 698 mg

**Menu Ideas: Pinwheel Dinner Rolls (page 82) and
Bacon-Lettuce and Tomato Salad (page 117) both
from "Busy People's Low-Fat Cookbook".**

Crockpot
Creations

Green Bean Soup

This is one of my favorite soups. I got the idea from a high fat soup served at one of the restaurants where I used to work.

1 (14-ounce) package low-fat smoked sausage (Healthy Choice)

¼ cup Butter Buds Sprinkles - dry

1 cup frozen chopped onion (or 1 medium onion-chopped)

1 pound fat-free, frozen, diced hash browns

1 pound frozen cut green beans

8 cups chicken stock (or 8 cups water with 8 chicken bouillon cubes dissolved)

4 bay leaves

♥ Put all ingredients in a crockpot and stir until well mixed.

♥ Cover.

♥ Cook on low for 8 to 10 hours or on high for 4 to 5 hours.

♥ Remove bay leaves before eating.

Yield: 12 (1-cup) servings

Calories: 94
Percent Fat Calories: 0%
Carbohydrate: 17 grams
Protein: 7 grams

Total Fat: 0 grams
Cholesterol: 15 mg
Dietary Fiber: 2 grams
Sodium: 1286 mg

Menu Ideas: Tossed salad and a sweet bread such as banana, cranberry or zucchini.

BEEF AND POTATO SOUP

*People who are "meat and potato"
eaters tend to especially like this soup.*

4 cups water
1 (16-ounce) bag frozen hash
browns (Southern-style)
1 cup frozen chopped onion
(or 1 medium onion -
chopped)
1 pound ground beef eye of
round

2 (4-ounce) cans mushroom
stems and pieces - do not
drain
1 (2.5-ounce) package dry
onion soup mix (2
packages per box)
1 (16-ounce) jar of your
favorite chunky salsa

♥ In a crockpot stir all ingredients until well mixed.

♥ Cover and cook on high for 4 hours or on low for 8 to 9 hours.

♥ If desired, salt and pepper to taste.

Yield: 11 (1-cup) servings

Calories: 131
Percent Fat Calories: 18%
Carbohydrate: 14 grams
Protein: 11 grams

Total Fat: 2 grams
Cholesterol: 23 mg
Dietary Fiber: 2 grams
Sodium: 876 mg

**Menu Ideas: Tossed salad and a favorite Aunt Millie's
bread with I Can't Believe It's Not Butter spray.**

Do everything in love.

First Corinthians 16:14

Crockpot
Creations

CHUNKY CROCKPOT CHILI

Budget
Friendly

Recipe

*Made with chunks of beef! The meat in
this hearty chili is tenderized as it cooks.*

1 pound beef for stew meat
(eye of round cut into
½-inch chunks)

1 (15-ounce) can Mexican-
style hot chili beans

1 (14½-ounce) can no-salt-
added diced tomatoes

1 (16-ounce) jar your
favorite thick and chunky
salsa (remember the
hotter the salsa the
hotter your chili is going
to be)

1 tablespoon sugar

♥ Stir all ingredients together in a crockpot until well mixed.

♥ Cover.

♥ Cook on low for 8 to 10 hours or on high for 4 to 5 hours.

♥ If desired, sprinkle with non-fat shredded cheddar cheese.
Let sit for 1 minute to allow cheese to melt.

Yield: 7 (1-cup) servings

Calories: 167
Percent Fat Calories: 19%
Carbohydrate: 16 grams
Protein: 18 grams

Total Fat: 3 grams
Cholesterol: 35 mg
Dietary Fiber: 3 grams
Sodium: 590 mg

**Menu Ideas: Sweet Corn Bread
(page 65 of "Busy People's Low-Fat Cookbook").**

*A true friend thinks
of you while others think
of themselves.*

Budget
Friendly
Recipe

GARLIC BEANS

*If you like Boston Market's
green beans, you'll love these.*

1 (1-pound) bag frozen
   green beans
4 ounces fresh mushrooms
   - sliced (for faster
   preparation, buy them
   pre-sliced in the produce
   section)
¼ cup Butter Buds
   Sprinkles - dry

1 tablespoon minced garlic
   (I use the kind in a jar)
   Light salt - to taste
   Black pepper - to taste
½ cup fat-free, reduced-
   sodium chicken or beef
   broth (or made from
   bouillon)

♥ Spray a crockpot with non-fat cooking spray.
♥ Put all ingredients into crockpot. Cover.
♥ Cook on high for 3 hours or on low for 6 hours.

Yield: 8 (½-cup) servings

Calories: 32
Percent Fat Calories: 0%
Carbohydrate: 8 grams
Protein: 2 grams

Total Fat: 0 grams
Cholesterol: 0 mg
Dietary Fiber: 2 grams
Sodium: 187 mg

Menu Ideas: Great side dish for any meal!

*Have you fifty friends?
It is not enough. Have you one enemy?
It is too much.*

Italian Proverb

Crockpot
Creations

Preparation Time: 3 minutes.

BACON GREEN BEANS

A delicious blend of lightly sweetened beans with a touch of tartness.

2 (1-pound) bags frozen cut green beans
⅓ cup Kikkoman Teriyaki Baste and Glaze (found in barbecue sauce section)

¼ cup fat-free Red Wine Vinegar Salad Dressing (Seven Seas)
1 (3-ounce) jar real bacon bits (I use Hormel)
1 cup onion - chopped (frozen chopped onions are fine)

♥ In a crockpot, stir all ingredients together until well mixed.

♥ Cover.

♥ Cook on high for 3½ to 4 hours or on low for 7 to 8 hours.

Yield: 12 (⅔-cup) servings

Calories: 68
Percent Fat Calories: 19%
Carbohydrate: 10 grams
Protein: 4 grams

Total Fat: 1 gram
Cholesterol: 5 mg
Dietary Fiber: 2 grams
Sodium: 476 mg

Menu Ideas: Any lean meat.

There is no other like your mother.

Crockpot Creations

Budget
Friendly

Recipe

TARRAGON CHICKEN AND POTATOES

*Sue Bucher, a friend, gave
me this recipe idea. I really like it!*

2 pounds boneless, skinless
  chicken breast
1 teaspoon dried tarragon
1 teaspoon minced garlic

¼ cup Butter Bud Sprinkles
  - dry - divided
5 large red skin potatoes
  Lite salt and ground
  pepper - optional

♥ Sprinkle chicken with dried tarragon, garlic and 2 table-spoons Butter Bud Sprinkles.

♥ Spray a crockpot with non-fat cooking spray.

♥ Place chicken in crockpot.

♥ Place potatoes on top of chicken. Sprinkle potatoes with remaining 2 tablespoons Butter Bud Sprinkles. Cover.

♥ Cook on low for 6½ to 8½ hours or on high for 3 to 4 hours.

♥ Lightly sprinkle chicken with lite salt and ground pepper before serving, if desired.

Yield: 5 servings (5 ounces cooked chicken and 1 potato each)

Calories: 303
Percent Fat Calories: 7%
Carbohydrate: 26 grams
Protein: 44 grams

Total Fat: 2 grams
Cholesterol: 105 mg
Dietary Fiber: 2 grams
Sodium: 413 mg

Menu Ideas: Sassy Slaw (page 109), Pinwheel Dinner Rolls (page 82), and Apple-Walnut Cookies (page 235) all in "Busy People's Low-Fat Cookbook".

Crockpot
Creations

Preparation Time: 10 minutes.

HOLIDAY PORK TENDERLOIN

*Excellent for the holidays instead
of the traditional ham or turkey.*

¼ cup cranberry sauce   2 pounds pork tenderloin
¼ cup apricot preserves

♥ Spray a crockpot with non-fat cooking spray.
♥ Mix cranberry sauce and apricot preserves until well blended.
♥ Spread glaze over pork tenderloin.
♥ Put in crockpot. Cover.
♥ Cook on low for 7½ to 9½ hours.

Yield: 8 (3-ounce) cooked servings

Calories: 177   Total Fat: 4 grams
Percent Fat Calories: 22%   Cholesterol: 67 mg
Carbohydrate: 10 grams   Dietary Fiber: 0 grams
Protein: 24 grams   Sodium: 54 mg

**Menu Ideas: Apricot Sweet Potatoes
(page 89) green beans and cornbread.**

*The prettiest thing
we can wear is a smile.*

Budget
Friendly

Recipe

CABBAGE ROLLS

Put the cabbage in the freezer until frozen.
(I do this days, even weeks ahead of time.) The leaves
will become soft, once thawed. No need to precook leaves.

1 (14-ounce) package fat-free kielbasa (Butterball) - cut into tiny ¼-inch pieces

1 cup cooked instant rice

¼ cup frozen or fresh chopped onion

2 egg whites

2 (10¾-ounce) cans reduced-sodium condensed tomato soup - do not make as directed on can - divided

8 large cabbage leaves - with stems cut off

♥ Spray a crockpot with non-fat cooking spray.

♥ Mix kielbasa, cooked rice, onion, egg whites and 2 tablespoons condensed soup until well mixed.

♥ Place ⅓ cup of mixture on each cabbage leaf.

♥ Roll up and secure with a toothpick.

♥ Place in crockpot.

♥ Pour remaining condensed soup over the top.

♥ Cover and cook on high for 2½ to 3 hours or on low for 5 to 6 hours or until cabbage is tender.

Yield: 4 servings (2 cabbage rolls each)

Calories: 381
Percent Fat Calories: 8%
Carbohydrate: 65 grams
Protein: 21 grams

Total Fat: 3 grams
Cholesterol: 43 mg
Dietary Fiber: 1 gram
Sodium: 1394 mg

Menu Ideas: Tossed salad and warm Vienna bread.

Crockpot
Creations

Preparation Time: 10 minutes or less.

POT ROAST - EXCELLENTE

Budget Friendly Recipe

*The ginger ale makes this tender and tasty!
I really like it! Don't worry, it is not sweet.*

2 pounds beef eye of round roast - all visible fat removed
4 cups ginger ale (not diet)

1 tablespoon minced garlic (I use the kind in a jar)
6 medium potatoes
3 large onions - cut into quarters

♥ Place roast in a crockpot.
♥ Pour ginger ale over roast.
♥ Stir garlic into ginger ale.
♥ Place potatoes and onions on top of roast.
♥ Cover. Cook on low for 7 to 9 hours or on high for 3½ to 4 hours.
♥ If desired, serve the juices on the side for dipping meat into.
♥ Salt and pepper to taste, if desired.

Yield: 6 servings (½ onion, 1 potato and 4 ounces cooked meat each)

Calories: 348
Percent Fat Calories: 18%
Carbohydrate: 34 grams
Protein: 37 grams

Total Fat: 7 grams
Cholesterol: 82 mg
Dietary Fiber: 4 grams
Sodium: 93 mg

Menu Ideas: Any green vegetable and a tossed salad with whole wheat dinner rolls.

Pork Dinner: Substitute pork tenderloin for the beef eye of round. Follow directions exactly.

Yield: 6 servings (½ onion, 1 potato and 4 ounces cooked meat each)

Calories: 330
Percent Fat Calories: 15%
Carbohydrate: 34 grams
Protein: 36 grams

Total Fat: 5 grams
Cholesterol: 98 mg
Dietary Fiber: 4 grams
Sodium: 89 mg

Crockpot Creations

TROPICAL PORK DINNER

This is one of my all time favorites! I absolutely love it!

2 pounds pork tenderloin
1 (20-ounce) can crushed pineapple
¼ cup honey
¼ cup apple cider vinegar
¼ cup packed dark brown sugar
4 large yams - washed (or 4 large sweet potatoes)

♥ Spray a crockpot with non-fat cooking spray.

♥ Place pork tenderloin in crockpot.

♥ Mix crushed pineapple, honey, vinegar and brown sugar together until well mixed. Spoon mixture over pork.

♥ Place yams on top of meat mixture. Cover. Cook on high for 3 to 4 hours or on low for 7 to 8 hours.

♥ Cut yams in half before serving. If desired, spoon a little sauce over cut yams and meat.

Yield: 8 servings (3 ounces cooked meat, ½ of a yam and 3 ounces of pineapple mixture)

Calories: 351
Percent Fat Calories: 11%
Carbohydrate: 53 grams
Protein: 26 grams
Total Fat: 4 grams
Cholesterol: 74 mg
Dietary Fiber: 5 grams
Sodium: 72 mg

Menu Ideas: Sassy Slaw (page 109 of "Busy People's Low-Fat Cookbook") and Hawaiian Rolls or cornbread.

Tropical Chicken Dinner: Make recipe exactly the same, but substitute 8 (4-ounce) boneless, skinless chicken breasts for the pork tenderloin.

Yield: 8 servings (3 ounces cooked meat, ½ of a yam and 3 ounces of pineapple mixture)

Calories: 340
Percent Fat Calories: 4%
Carbohydrate: 53 grams
Protein: 28 grams
Total Fat: 2 grams
Cholesterol: 66 mg
Dietary Fiber: 5 grams
Sodium: 89 mg

Crockpot Creations

SAUSAGE AND ACORN SQUASH

To prepare this recipe faster, I mix ingredients and fill squash with my hands. A terrific autumn meal!

1 (14-ounce) package fat-free smoked sausage - cut into tiny ¼- ½-inch chunks

¼ teaspoon ground dried sage

1 tablespoon Butter Buds Sprinkles - dry

⅓ cup packed dark brown sugar

2 acorn squash - cut in half (vertically) and seeded

1 cup water

♥ In a medium bowl mix sausage, sage, Butter Buds and brown sugar together until all of the sausage is well coated with seasonings.

♥ Fill each squash half (4 halves total) heaping full.

♥ Wrap each stuffed squash separately in foil.

♥ Put water in bottom of a crockpot.

♥ Place wrapped squash in crockpot. It's fine to set on top of each other (if you need to).

♥ Cook on high for 4 hours or on low for 8 to 9 hours.

Yield: 4 servings (1 stuffed half each)

Calories: 262
Percent Fat Calories: 0%
Carbohydrate: 52 grams
Protein: 17 grams

Total Fat: 0 grams
Cholesterol: 43 mg
Dietary Fiber: 3 grams
Sodium: 1267 mg

***Menu Ideas: Applesauce
(cinnamon-flavored or
peach-flavored would be great!)
and cornbread muffins.***

PIGS OUT OF THE BLANKET

If you like pigs in the blanket you'll like this! It's just as delicious and a lot less time consuming to prepare.

1 pound ground beef eye of round

2 cups dry instant long grain white rice

1 (16-ounce) jar of your favorite salsa (remember, the spicier your salsa the spicier your dish)

2 cups V8 juice

1 (16-ounce) package cole slaw mix (found in your produce section, it has cabbage and carrots)

2 (14.5-ounce) cans no-salt-added stewed tomatoes

♥ Spray a 4-quart crockpot with non-fat cooking spray.

♥ Mix* all ingredients except stewed tomatoes until well blended in the crockpot. (Remove any large pieces of cabbage and discard.)

♥ Cover. Cook on high for 4 hours.

♥ When ready to serve, microwave stewed tomatoes until fully heated. Evenly pour stewed tomatoes over each serving.

*I find it's easiest to mix with my hands.

Yield: 6 (1-cup) servings

Calories: 313
Percent Fat Calories: 11%
Carbohydrate: 42 grams
Protein: 21 grams

Total Fat: 3 grams
Cholesterol: 41 mg
Dietary Fiber: 4 grams
Sodium: 633 mg

**Menu Ideas: This is a meal in itself.
Sugar-free Jell-O or a piece of fruit, if desired.**

Crockpot
Creations

STUFFED GREEN PEPPERS

Budget
Friendly

Recipe

Talk about quick to prepare.
It doesn't get any easier than this.

4 large fresh green peppers
1 pound ground beef eye of round (or ground turkey breast)
2 cups dry instant long grain white rice

2 cups V8 juice, mild picante flavor (or regular flavor is fine)
2 (14.5-ounce) cans no-salt-added sliced, stewed tomatoes

♥ Spray a crockpot with non-fat cooking spray. Set aside.

♥ Cut tops off green peppers and discard. Clean out insides of green peppers. Set aside.

♥ In a bowl, mix ground beef eye of round, rice and V8 juice together.

♥ Stuff peppers with meat/rice mixture.

♥ Arrange stuffed peppers in crockpot.

♥ Arrange sliced, stewed tomatoes on top of and around peppers in bottom of crockpot.

♥ Cover. Cook on high for 4 hours or on low for 8 to 9 hours.

♥ When serving, cut each pepper in half vertically. Lay each pepper on a plate on its side with beef and rice mixture facing up.

♥ Spoon stewed tomatoes and the juices in the bottom of the crockpot over each pepper.

Yield: 4 servings

With beef eye of round:

Calories: 447
Percent Fat Calories: 11%
Carbohydrate: 63 grams
Protein: 31 grams

Total Fat: 5 grams
Cholesterol: 61 mg
Dietary Fiber: 7 grams
Sodium: 403 mg

(Stuffed Green Peppers continued)

With turkey breast:

Calories: 423
Percent Fat Calories: 3%
Carbohydrate: 63 grams
Protein: 34 grams

Total Fat: 1 gram
Cholesterol: 77 mg
Dietary Fiber: 7 grams
Sodium: 394 mg

Menu Ideas: A meal in itself. If desired a side dish of green beans and dessert such as Cookies and Cream Three-Layer Dessert (on page 190).

Every good gift and every perfect gift is from above.

James 1:17

Crockpot Creations

HOMESTEAD HAM STEAKS
(OR HOMESTEAD PORK TENDERLOIN)
(OR HOMESTEAD CHICKEN BREAST)

Budget
Friendly
Recipe

The mouth-watering flavors of these
aromatic spices make a fantastic fall feast!

1 tablespoon mustard
1 teaspoon ground allspice
1¼ cups orange marmalade - divided
8 (⅓-inch thick) lean ham steaks (about 2 pounds)

4 cups dry instant white rice
1 (14.5-ounce) can sliced carrots - drained

♥ Mix mustard, allspice and ¾ cup orange marmalade together. Spread glaze on each ham steak. Stack steaks in a crockpot. Cover.

♥ Cook on high for 3½ to 4 hours or on low for 7 to 8 hours.

♥ Once fully cooked, drain juices from crockpot. (Juices will measure about 1 cup.) Add enough water to drained juices to measure 4 cups of liquid and pour into a 2-quart (or larger) saucepan.

♥ Bring liquid to a full boil over high heat.

♥ Gently stir in rice, remaining ½ cup orange marmalade and carrots. Cover and remove from heat.

♥ Let stand 5 minutes or until liquid is absorbed. Fluff with a fork.

♥ Serve rice mixture with ham steaks.

Yield: 8 servings (4 ounces meat and ¾ cup rice each)

Calories: 443
Percent Fat Calories: 10%
Carbohydrate: 73 grams
Protein: 27 grams

Total Fat: 5 grams
Cholesterol: 51 mg
Dietary Fiber: 1 gram
Sodium: 1591 mg

Menu Ideas: Garlic Beans (page 239).

Homestead Pork Tenderloin: Substitute 2 pounds pork tenderloin for the ham. Make recipe exactly the same.

Yield: 8 servings (3 ounces cooked meat and ³/₄ cup rice each)

Calories: 441
Percent Fat Calories: 8%
Carbohydrate: 73 grams
Protein: 28 grams

Total Fat: 4 grams
Cholesterol: 74 mg
Dietary Fiber: 1 gram
Sodium: 209 mg

Homestead Chicken Breast: Substitute 2 pounds boneless, skinless chicken breast for the ham. Make recipe exactly the same.

Yield: 8 servings (3 ounces cooked meat and ³/₄ cup rice each)

Calories: 430
Percent Fat Calories: 3%
Carbohydrate: 73 grams
Protein: 31 grams

Total Fat: 2 grams
Cholesterol: 66 mg
Dietary Fiber: 1 gram
Sodium: 226 mg

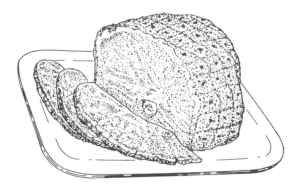

Crockpot Creations

PORK ROAST

An old time favorite made a lot easier!

2 (16-ounce) bags frozen vegetables for stew (I use Freshlike)
1 (14.5-ounce) can no-salt-added stewed tomatoes
1 (10.5-ounce) can Healthy Choice cream of celery soup

1 teaspoon dried thyme (or 2 teaspoons fresh thyme)
1½ pounds pork tenderloin
⅓ cup flour
¼ cup water

♥ Spray a crockpot with non-fat cooking spray.

♥ In a crockpot, mix vegetables, stewed tomatoes, soup and thyme together until well blended.

♥ Push pork to the bottom and the sides of crockpot.

♥ Cover. Cook on low for 8 to 10 hours or on high 4 to 5 hours.

♥ With a slotted spoon, remove vegetables and pork. Leave juice in crockpot and turn crockpot on high.

♥ In a small bowl, mix flour and water together to make a thick paste.

♥ Stir paste into juices in crockpot until well blended.

♥ Cover and cook on high for 5 minutes, or until thick.

♥ If desired, season to taste with garlic salt and black pepper.

♥ Place cooked pork and vegetables on a platter. Serve with the gravy on the side.

Yield: 6 servings

Calories: 298
Percent Fat Calories: 15%
Carbohydrate: 34 grams
Protein: 27 grams

Total Fat: 5 grams
Cholesterol: 76 mg
Dietary Fiber: 4 grams
Sodium: 348 mg

Menu Ideas: Rye bread and Garlic Beans (page 239).

SAUERKRAUT AND PORK

Even my children (who do not like sauerkraut) like this meal. It's not strong or overpowering like a lot of sauerkraut entrées are.

1½ pounds pork tenderloin steaks (or buy a pork tenderloin roast and cut into eight 1-inch steaks)
1 (16-ounce) bag fresh whole baby carrots
½ cup frozen chopped onion (I use Ore Ida)

1 (14-ounce) can sauerkraut - do not drain
2 medium Granny Smith apples - chopped into tiny pieces
1 tablespoon packed brown sugar

♥ Spray a crockpot with non-fat cooking spray.

♥ Lay meat slices on bottom of crockpot, top with carrots. Stir frozen chopped onion, sauerkraut, apples and brown sugar together. Spread sauerkraut mixture over pork and carrots. Cover.

♥ Cook on high for 4 to 5 hours or low for 8 to 9 hours.

Yield: 8 servings

Calories: 168
Percent Fat Calories: 18%
Carbohydrate: 16 grams
Protein: 19 grams

Total Fat: 3 grams
Cholesterol: 55 mg
Dietary Fiber: 4 grams
Sodium: 418 mg

Menu Ideas: Serve over mashed potatoes. (Potatoes A-La-Larry which is in my first book "Down Home Cookin' Without the Down Home Fat" page 60, is a great, fast and easy mashed potato recipe that'll be perfect with this meal.)

Crockpot Creations

HOLIDAY PORK BARBECUE

The cranberry sauce in this smooth and lightly sweetened barbecue is a delicious and unique twist just right for holiday meals!

1 (16-ounce) can jellied cranberry sauce
1 cup honey mustard barbecue sauce (your favorite brand)

2 pounds pork tenderloin (you can substitute chicken breast or extra lean ham)
8 medium potatoes

♥ Spray a crockpot with non-fat cooking spray.

♥ In crockpot, mix cranberry sauce and barbecue sauce together until well blended.

♥ With a knife, make little cuts about ½-inch deep around the outside of the pork. Place meat in crockpot and cover with sauce.

♥ Place potatoes on top of meat.

♥ Cook on low for 8 to 9 hours or on high for 4 hours.

Note: If desired, in order for the meat to absorb more flavor, put your meat and sauce in a zip lock bag a few days ahead of time.

Yield: 8 (3-ounces cooked meat and one potato) servings

With pork:

Calories: 361
Percent Fat Calories: 10%
Carbohydrate: 55 grams
Protein: 26 grams

Total Fat: 4 grams
Cholesterol: 74 mg
Dietary Fiber: 2 grams
Sodium: 400 mg

With chicken breast:

Calories: 350
Percent Fat Calories: 4%
Carbohydrate: 55 grams
Protein: 29 grams

Total Fat: 2 grams
Cholesterol: 66 mg
Dietary Fiber: 2 grams
Sodium: 417 mg

(Holiday Pork Barbecue continued)

With extra lean ham:

Calories: 361
Percent Fat Calories: 13%
Carbohydrate: 55 grams
Protein: 23 grams

Total Fat: 5 grams
Cholesterol: 43 mg
Dietary Fiber: 2 grams
Sodium: 1766 mg

Menu idea: Once meal is completely cooked, cut potatoes in half. Spoon sauce over potatoes and meat when serving. Serve with steamed asparagus and fresh rolls.

Honesty is the first chapter in the book of wisdom.

Thomas Jefferson

Crockpot Creations

Preparation Time: 10 minutes or less.

SCALLOP POTATOES AND SAUSAGE

I love these! They're super creamy!
(Please note, although the potatoes are not cut in the traditional manner of slices, this recipe is every bit as good. . .if not better than the traditional recipe).

1 pint fat-free half & half (I use Land O Lakes)
⅓ cup all-purpose flour
1 tablespoon Butter Buds Sprinkles - dry
½ cup frozen chopped onion (or ½ cup fresh chopped onion)

2 (14-ounce) packages Butterball fat-free smoked sausage - cut into ¼-inch bite-size pieces
1 (2-pound) bag frozen, fat-free shredded hash browns (I use Mr. Dells)

♥ Spray a crockpot with non-fat cooking spray.

♥ With a whisk briskly stir half & half, flour and Butter Buds together in a crockpot until flour is completely dissolved.

♥ With large spoon stir in onions, smoked sausage and shredded hash browns until well mixed.

♥ Cover. Cook on high for 3½ to 4 hours or on low for 8 to 9 hours.

♥ Pepper to taste if desired.

Yield: 8 (1-cup) servings

Calories: 257
Percent Fat Calories: 0%
Carbohydrate: 44 grams
Protein: 22 grams
Total Fat: 0 grams
Cholesterol: 43 mg
Dietary Fiber: 2 grams
Sodium: 1276 mg

Menu Ideas: Spring Salad (page 120) and Spring Asparagus (page 134, both recipes are from "Busy People's Low-Fat Cookbook").

Scallop Potatoes and Ham: Prepare exactly the same, but substitute 2 pounds extra lean ham cut into bite-size pieces for the smoked sausage.

Yield: 8 (1-cup) servings

Calories: 290　　　　　　　Total Fat: 5 grams
Percent Fat Calories: 16%　Cholesterol: 43 mg
Carbohydrate: 34 grams　　Dietary Fiber: 2 grams
Protein: 28 grams　　　　　Sodium: 1535 mg

Cheesy Scallop Potatoes and Ham: After Scallop Potatoes and Ham recipe is completely cooked, stir in 5 slices fat-free American cheese (Kraft or Borden brand). Cut cheese into tiny pieces before stirring into dish.

Yield: 8 (1-cup) servings

Calories: 306　　　　　　　Total Fat: 5 grams
Percent Fat Calories: 15%　Cholesterol: 46 mg
Carbohydrate: 35 grams　　Dietary Fiber: 2 grams
Protein: 30 grams　　　　　Sodium: 1648 mg

Cheesy Scallop Potatoes and Sausage: After Scallop Potatoes and Sausage recipe is completely cooked, stir in 5 slices fat-free American Cheese (Kraft or Borden brand). Cut cheese into tiny pieces before stirring into dish.

Yield: 8 (1-cup) servings

Calories: 272　　　　　　　Total Fat: 0 grams
Percent Fat Calories: 0%　Cholesterol: 46 mg
Carbohydrate: 46 grams　　Dietary Fiber: 2 grams
Protein: 25 grams　　　　　Sodium: 1388 mg

Crockpot Creations

GREEN BEAN STEW

When out for the day, I have a cozy feeling knowing this flavorful combination, with its tantalizing aroma, will greet our arrival home.

1 (14-ounce) package fat-free smoked sausage - diced (I use Healthy Choice)

4 cups Health Valley fat-free, no-salt-added beef broth (or 4 beef bouillon cubes dissolved in 4 cups water)

2 (10-ounce) packages frozen cut green beans (or one 16-ounce bag)

4 medium to large potatoes - thinly sliced (or 1½ pounds frozen, diced, fat-free hash browns potatoes)

1 medium onion - chopped (or 1 cup frozen chopped onion)

½ teaspoon ground black pepper

2 tablespoons Butter Buds Sprinkles - dry (do not add water)

♥ Stir everything into a crockpot and cover.

♥ Cook on low for 8 to 9 hours or on high for 4 to 4½ hours. Make sure potatoes are covered with broth while cooking.

Yield: 10 (1-cup) servings

Calories: 128
Percent Fat Calories: 0%
Carbohydrate: 23 grams
Protein: 11 grams

Total Fat: 0 grams
Cholesterol: 17 mg
Dietary Fiber: 3 grams
Sodium: 573 mg

Menu Idea: Sour dough bread or rolls.

Crockpot
Creations

HOT FUDGIE CAKE

*Super moist! Super delicious! I like to whip this
up quickly before church. When I get home from church
it's an extra special treat everyone loves to devour!
Many say it is their favorite of my desserts.*

3 cups skim milk
1 (5-ounce) box chocolate
  cook and serve pudding
  mix (Jell-O brand) - dry
  (Do not make as
  directed on box.)

1 (18.25-ounce) box super
  moist chocolate fudge
  cake mix - dry (Betty
  Crocker brand)
1⅓ cups water
½ cup applesauce
6 egg whites

♥ Spray a 3½-quart crockpot with non-fat cooking spray.

♥ Mix skim milk with dry chocolate pudding mix in crockpot until
completely dissolved with whisk.

♥ In a medium bowl, mix dry cake mix, water, applesauce and
egg whites using a whisk for 2 minutes or until well blended.

♥ Very gently pour cake batter into uncooked pudding mixture
in crockpot. DO NOT STIR!

♥ Cover and cook on high for 2½ hours.

♥ Serve hot with a dab of Cool Whip Free.

♥ If desired, after 2½ hours of cooking, just unplug crockpot.
It'll stay warm and delicious for hours. It travels well to
potlucks or social gatherings.

Yield: 15 servings

Calories: 204
Percent Fat Calories: 14%
Carbohydrate: 39 grams
Protein: 4 grams

Total Fat: 3 grams
Cholesterol: 1 mg
Dietary Fiber: 1 gram
Sodium: 302 mg

Crockpot
Creations

Menu Ideas: Potlucks and special dinners.

Notes

Index

263

D

F

G

H

Index

Index

S

Salad Dressings

Salads

Sandwiches

Sauerkraut

Sausage (also see Pork)

ABOUT THE AUTHOR

Dawn Hall is also the author of two other award-winning low-fat cookbooks. "Down Home Cookin' Without the Down Home Fat," was selected as "1996 Best Book of the Year in the Category of Cooking" by North American Bookdealers Exchange and one of "Ohio's Best of the Best Cookbooks." The original "Busy People's Low-Fat Cookbook" received a certificate of merit from Writer's Digest and won "1998 Best Book of the Year in the Category of Cooking by North American Book Dealers Exchange.

As an accomplished aerobic instructor and facilitator for W.O.W. (Watching Our Weight - low-fat living class) Dawn feels like she was born watching her weight. She is a successful recovering, compulsive over eater and food addict; for which she is very grateful!! Dawn walks her talk and is living proof "you can have your cake and eat it too" without eating and weeping!

She strongly believes her talent for creating extremely low-fat, mouth-watering foods that are made quickly and effortlessly is a gift from God. Therefore, 10% of the author's profits go to "Solid Rock" an inner-city outreach program for children and teens with hopes of building a strong moral foundation for our future generation.

As a popular inspirational speaker and veteran talk show guest, Dawn has appeared on "The 700 Club," "CBN," "Woman to Woman," "Good Morning A.M." along with numerous other T.V. and radio programs nationwide.

To contact the author call, write or fax:

Cozy Homestead Publishing

c/o Dawn Hall

5425 S. Fulton-Lucas Road

Swanton, OH 43558

(419) 826-2665 or Fax (419) 826-2700

Cookbook Order Form

These COOKBOOKS make GREAT Gifts! Stock up and keep some on hand (for those last minute gifts).

Look at chart below for cost of book.

Qty.	Item	Cost Per Book	Total
	"2nd Serving of Busy People's Low-Fat Cookbook"		
	"Busy People's Low-Fat Cookbook"		
	"Down Home Cookin Without the Down Home Fat"		
	OH residents add 6.25% Sales Tax per book		
	Add $2 per book-shipping & handling (&3 if only 1 book)		
	TOTAL		

Fill out and send this order form with payment to:

Cozy Homestead Publishing
5425 S. Fulton-Lucas Road, Swanton, OH 43558

VISA, Mastercard, and Discover are Welcome

Call Toll Free 1-888-436-9646

Name _____

Address _____

City _____ State _____ Zip _____

Phone number _____

Credit Card/Acct.# _____ Exp. Date _____

Signature _____

DISCOUNTS

Any combination of books	Cost per book	Total cost for all books	2 or more books equal $2 per bk. shipping	Total costs
1	$15.95	$15.95	$3.00*	$18.95
2	$12.50	$25.00	$4.00	$29.00
3 or more	$10.00	$30.00	$6.00	$36.00

*if only 1 book

3 or more books are $10.00 each plus $2.00 per book shipping & handling.

ALSO AVAILABLE AT YOUR FAVORITE BOOKSTORE.

If you would like to know of future recipe books written by Dawn just fill out the card below. When her next book comes out we'll be sure to let you know!

Name _____

Address _____

City _____ State _____ Zip _____

What I liked most about your book:

_____

_____

_____

What I'd like to see more of:

_____

_____

_____

Thanks for your encouragement!
God Bless & Good Eatin's!
Love,
Dawn

Mail to: Cozy Homestead Publishers, Inc.
5425 S. Fulton-Lucas Rd.
Swanton, OH 43558

If you've created your own fast and easy,
extremely low fat, and delicious recipe mail to:

Dawn Hall
c/o Cozy Homestead Publishers
5425 S. Fulton-Lucas Rd.
Swanton, Ohio 43558

Each recipe published will have a write-up
about its originator next to it.

For information on:

Dawn Hall's
other
award-winning
low-fat
cookbooks

call toll-free
(888) 436-9646

"Down Home
Cookin' Without the
Down Home Fat"

"Busy People's
Low-Fat
Cookbook"

Fund-raising Information

These books are available at quantity discounts with bulk purchases for business, educational, fund-raising or sales promotional use. For more information write, call or fax:

Cozy Homestead Publishing, Inc.
5425 S. Fulton-Lucas Road
Swanton, OH 43558
Phone: (419) 826-COOK (2665)
Fax: (419) 826-2700

"Busy People's Low-Fat Cookbook"

"Down Home Cookin' Without the Down Home Fat"

"2nd Serving of Busy People's Low-Fat Cookbook"

282

About Solid Rock

Few things have given me greater joy in life than knowing our family is trying to make a positive difference in the inner city of Toledo by being involved with the Solid Rock program. With a hands-on involvement Pastor Keith and his wonderful wife Shannon focus on the needs of the central city, crossing over both racial and economic barriers.

Through their Kids Church program for children and their youth group for teens they are establishing a moral foundation for the future generation based on Biblical principles.

We are in constant need of bus drivers to transport children to the programs, as well as more volunteers to help in many other areas. Last but not least, child sponsors are needed.

For information contact: Keith Stepp, Solid Rock, 1630 Broadway, Toledo, Ohio 43609 or call: 419-244-7020.

10% of my profits from this book are going towards Toledo's Solid Rock Outreach Program. On behalf of all the children, thank you very much for your support!

Sincerely,

Dawn

Notes

Notes

Notes

Notes

_____

_____

_____

_____

_____

_____

_____

_____

_____

_____

_____

_____

_____

_____

_____

_____

_____

_____

_____

_____

_____

Notes